AN INSIDE JOB

An Inside Job

A practical guide to finding your true self

ROSE MONACO

Believe The Best Is Yet To Come

I dedicate this book to my beautiful children Christopher and Danielle – "A mothers masterpiece is her children". Also to Helen, my friend, my truth, and my kick in the pants! I miss you x

Dream

All you need is a DREAM.
BELIEVE in that dream.
TRUST in who you are.
Allow yourself to EVOLVE and
BECOME the you that you have always wanted to be.

This is your life, your dream, your creation.
Make it magnificent!

Publishing Details:
Publisher: Believe The Best Is Yet To Come
ISBN: 978-0-6485988-1-7 (Paperback)
ISBN: 978-0-6485988-0-0 (Hardback)
ISBN: 978-0-6485988-2-4 (ePub)

Front cover photo: Alice Mole, Paper Hat Studio
Cover layout: Pickawoowoo Publishing Group
Automated composition layout: Pickawoowoo Publishing Group
Editing: Eddie Albrecht, Pickawoowoo Publishing Group
Artwork / Line drawings: Sean Nicholls Illustrations
Printing and channel distribution: Lightning Source / Ingram

Author contact:
Facebook: Rose Monaco / Believe The Best Is Yet To Come
Website: www.rosemonaco.com
www.believethebestisyetocome.com

Contents

Preface

Let me tell you a little bit about myself. I am a first generation Australian from Italian parents, an only child and a big believer in having the power to create your tomorrows. I am a survivor of childhood sexual abuse. I am a warrior of life and believe that no matter how many times I fell, I was worth getting up and fighting for. I believe in a greater power and the beautiful angels that guide me.

My connection with the angels began for me as a young child, when I sat alone in church before the school gates would open and I asked the angels why my 'uncle' was hurting me. I was a five year old who had to grow up very quickly but my angels have been with me from as far as I can remember. I would talk to them in my mind and heart, and as soon as I called for them, they came. I would either see them, hear them or feel them around me. Through my most difficult times, their presence gave me what I needed, which was love and comfort. They would help me accept what was happening to me, and later in life I realised it all happened for me so that I could be the person I am today. Even when the abuse was happening, my angels would embrace me and take me away from the trauma of it all so I could be as 'normal' as I could be. The repeated abuse began at the tender age of 3½ and didn't end until I was eight.

The angels made me feel that I was not alone, especially at times where I was in the dark. No matter where I was going in life, if I saw an angel then I knew I was going the right way. A picture, a statue, a name, anything that meant 'angel' to me. They were my sign posts pointing me in the direction that led me to where I am now.

Over the years I followed several angel signs to many people who had lessons to teach me. One was a tarot reader in Melbourne who put me firmly on the path to where I am now. I had been looking for someone to guide me at that time as I was very lost and felt like I was walking around in circles. When I was guided to her, I looked for an angel sign so I knew I was in the right place. When she opened the door, she looked at me strangely and asked me to take a seat in her lounge as she was still with another client. I was feeling apprehensive and nervous, worried if I was in the right place. As I sat on her couch, I looked up and a giant angel portrait was before me and I knew in my heart this was a safe place. As I sat with the tarot reader, her first words were, 'Why are you here? The angels already work through you.' She then proceeded to tell me that I wasn't there to get a reading, I was there for my next step. She said, 'I am being told to teach you tarot as quick as I can as you are going home and your angels are wanting you to do this as you will help many.' I had never thought of reading the tarot, but it wasn't just about the tarot, it was about working with the angels in a different way. So instead of only hearing them and trying to work out what they were telling me, as I was helping others, they gave me this tool through the cards so I could help others.

From that point, my journey of self-discovery began as the angels started to work intensely with me and I was guided to many teachers, and many were guided to me. To help others, I was told I had to heal myself first. I couldn't just keep starting from this 'now' point, as the past continued to drag me back and then sabotage my desperate want to move forward. The angels told me I couldn't keep helping others whilst I wore a mask to hide my pain from my past. I had to go back and find the little girl who was left behind and rewire my belief system so that my beginning from this point wouldn't be tainted by my past but enriched by it.

I continued to work with the tarot and the angels guided me to read the tarot from my heart and not the book. I trusted my angels but this was a lesson in trusting myself, my ability and my gift. The angels told me they would send people to me who were at a crossroad in their lives, and I would help them find their way back. I wasn't your traditional tarot reader, but more a life coach, helping others to believe and trust in themselves to know the direction they needed to take. The more I healed myself and trusted the universal guidance, the stronger my intuition became and the answers were clearer.

Through this time, I still felt the pain of my ongoing lessons, and at times I fell to my knees, but I trusted that there was a purpose to all of this. Sometimes, it was so hard to get back on my feet again but a little voice inside me would say, 'I believe in you'. I knew that was me. As I grew stronger, so did my inner voice. I began to understand life and how it worked, and how I responded to it. I understood that life was like an elevator that moved me through my emotions. Sometimes it would lift me up where I would feel joy and peace, and at other times drop me into a hole of despair. I realised that I always had a choice of how I dealt with my emotions but I needed to understand the levels between joy and peace, and the hole of despair.

As I became more in tune with who I really was, the levels became clearer and I could see the vicious circle I had been in for most of my life. I knew that I didn't want to let my past ruin my future anymore, and I didn't want my inner critic to control the trust I was gaining in myself. My past had already stolen so much from me, and I wasn't prepared to give it any more power to rob me of the precious time I have. Instead, I wanted to find that little girl again who I had left behind, help her out of the dark and love her in the way she always deserved to be loved. I wanted to feel more in control of my life, and to own it and not let anyone else tell me who I am and what I need to do anymore. I placed my trust in the universe and my angels to help me through my biggest lesson of all – to follow my own intuition and guidance so I could become the leader in my life. I was willing to go on the important journey of finding my true authentic self. What a journey it has been and how privileged I am to be in a place I had always dreamt of being in. Life blesses me every day.

If you're a seeker like me, this journey will take you to places inside yourself where you will find you – the real you. The you that got lost along the way in life and wants to be found again! This book will take you on your own journey of self-discovery. I will not lead you, I will walk with you, step by step as you find yourself in this book. You are not alone; you never have been. Take this step and give yourself the gift of you.

Chapter 1

INTRODUCTION

Life is truly beautiful; it is so precious yet fragile, and it can be unpredictable at times but remember that each day is a gift.

In the past, I went through life wondering why others had what I wanted and questioned why obstacles were always in my way. I was always riddled with guilt at the thought of putting myself first, as I was taught not to be selfish, so I always put other people's needs, wants and opinions before my own. Their needs were always more important than mine. However, if I could go back, knowing what I know now, I would have been much more gentle with the little girl who felt invisible, thinking she was insignificant and unloved.

We are not here to be either a failure or perfection; we are here to be whoever we want to be. We are here to experience what life has to offer.

It is our response to these experiences that control our next step. We can either push against what's happening to us, or we can see the pattern and work with it.

We are actually the ones who are always creating what happens to us next – we create our future experiences. So if we can do this, why would we want to create situations we don't want? Only you can make changes that will create a better tomorrow for yourself. It all starts with you!

In this book, you will read about the five levels of awareness, how to recognise each one and how to work within them. You will learn to appreciate each level, what it offers you and see the opportunity it holds. When we need to change, it may come to us as a person, a loss, a gift, an obstacle, or a closed door. We can accept change as it opens new doors and creates many opportunities. However, when you resist the change, it can give you the sense of being stuck or that you are going backwards or not moving at all. For example, I was in a relationship for many years and I knew it was not healthy for me or my children, yet I was afraid to make the change because of what it could potentially mean for me. My lack of confidence and fear of the future kept me stuck in limbo. Then a number of years ago, on a cold July day there was a moment that presented itself to me, where I felt intimidated, afraid and truly alone. I could have chosen to stay in the relationship and remain lonely, anxious and empty, but I chose to change and open a new door.

Think about this; what happens *to* you is really what happens *for* you. So when I felt intimidated and afraid, I felt it was happening to me and it made me feel like a victim, but it was actually the pivotal point that brought me change. So in reality, it was happening for me, for my greater good. I was able to see the relationship for what it was and I knew at that point that I deserved better for myself, even if it meant I was to be on my own.

When you fight against change, the more disillusioned you will become. Doubt, fear and your inner critic disempowers you and you are further away from where you really want to be. You know this isn't how you want it to be, and at some point in your life you ask yourself if this is all life is. The thought of change may bring fear, so you hesitate to do anything to unsettle your life any more than it already feels.

The obstacle in your way to happiness is you, and only you can change that. Once you understand *why* you are in your situation, you can then *see* it so much clearer and bring in the change that you need to shift that negative 'why' into a positive action. We can choose to stay in a victim mentality or bring out an internal warrior who proves to you that you have the strength to make anything happen in your life, and the 'why' becomes a challenge and not a setback.

I have been very blessed to help many through these teachings and I hope this book resonates with you and helps you to understand, accept and honour where you are in your life. I hope it also gives you the guidelines to create the life you truly want with intent and purpose.

So where did it begin? About five years ago I was in a very robotic phase of my life and I was feeling empty and hollow. I was in a relationship that I felt alone in, I had an injury that made me feel broken and impacted my life, my past continued to haunt me, a lot was going on in my family that I didn't know what to do about and in amongst this I was lost and I didn't know who I really was and where I was going. I had been told many times by colleagues that I would write a book. I didn't know what the book would be about, and I tried to write many times but I could never get past the first page. I decided that if I was meant to write a book, I would know about it when it was time.

One day, I received a clear vision of a very wise man who I was told about previously. (See Image). He had a long beard, long hair and deep comforting eyes. I had been told that this man would come forward to give me a book I had written before. I would know what this book was about when it was time. So when I had the vision, I wondered if it was him. He said nothing to me other than appearing before me. Even though I was surprised by this, it did leave me wondering if he was 'the wise man' I was told about previously. I was given no book at that time, I waited and waited but gave up thinking that maybe it was a vision of something else. At the time, I let it go, feeling a little deflated. It took six months before this book was given to me in a dream that would change my life as I knew it.

In this dream, I was coaching a class and I remembered everything I was teaching. All the levels were behind me on a screen and everything I was saying made sense! I was buzzing from all I'd learnt in this dream. I jumped out of bed, grabbed a pile of paper and started to write it all down. My son was up and wondering what I was doing writing frantically but I didn't want to forget what I had heard. I understood the concept and I made it part of my everyday living. I wanted to see if such an understanding would help me in my life.

I was taken from the foundation up, level by level in my everyday life. The more I understood the concepts, the more I knew I had to be prepared for change as I could feel my mind and heart working together for the first time. I knew I couldn't keep existing as I had been for most of my life because I knew I deserved more. My heart and my head were in sync and both were working together to help me release all the negativity I had in my mind, my heart and my soul. As the negative was being removed it was being filled with love.

I was a puzzle being put back together. I knew I had to have a start point, and for me, a lot stemmed from my abuse from the age of 3½. I had to find the precious little girl who got lost in a world she didn't understand or feel worthy of so I could change my life from that point. I'd tried many times to change my life but my past pain kept dragging me back, so I knew if I was to do this properly I had to start from the beginning where it really began. There were pieces I didn't even know or recognise but as I changed, the pieces began to fit. I began to see how the actions of others taught an innocent girl a 'warped' idea of what life and love was all about. A little girl who had no idea what was right or wrong but was being shown where she sat in this big world. She was taught that she was there for others, and definitely not for herself. She was there to be used when needed and abandoned when not. Happiness to her was going to school, where she would be spoken to, even if it was to be bullied. Actions made her introverted at home, but at school she could be a child, playful and amusing. She talked a lot and was funny! Even got in trouble for it, but at school, she was heard and accepted. Her sense of humour made people like her, and she so desperately wanted to be liked. She thought if she was liked, maybe she wouldn't be so easily disposed of. Or so she thought. I had to find this little girl to help her see what life really was about, and to help her believe she was worthy of standing in her strength and having the life she fantasised about through the TV screen and books.

When I soul-searched to find her inside me, I had a vision of her huddled in a ball in a dark room, forgotten, scared, unloved and fragile. I nurtured her and I had to earn her trust so she felt safe. I loved her unconditionally and slowly helped her to believe in herself so she could come out of the dark space when she felt it was safe. I slowly rewired all she had known; the fear, rejection, insecurity, her nightmares, her self-loathing, the ridicule and mistrust from others and the loneliness – I dealt with each of these one at a time. This took a long time as I had been living and feeling this way for over 45 years. It broke me as I realised how I had tried to hide and forget her. I'd placed myself in a cocoon so I didn't have to go back there again and feel the pain of all that had happened. I ignored her needs, wants and dreams as if they were insignificant and unattainable. If I thought of her I would be overcome with tears, guilt and pain for all she had endured at such a young age because I never understood what to do to help her. All I had learned was that others were much more important than me. I looked for all she wanted in other people. I went on their paths and not my own. This was the foundation of my life, where I built my understanding of what I thought life and love were all about. I didn't understand what a foundation of healthy self-love, trust and belief in myself looked or felt like. Not until I noticed the words I was telling myself, the actions I was taking to sabotage my life and the importance I placed on others' opinions of me, did I grasp what a mess I was creating of my life.

I didn't realise how the conditioning of my childhood, my religion, old family traditions and insecurities moulded me into who I was and what big expectations I had of myself. I built myself around others and not myself – their expectations not my own – like I didn't matter. My foundation was poorly created from the start.

The levels in this book helped me to find the true me, the authentic me, the *me* I had always wanted to be. I had to go back, recreate my foundation and finally step onto my own true path. I have a much greater understanding and this has changed my life and how I see it. I have lived each level one step at a time, feeling all the emotions and frustrations of breaking away from my old way of thinking that wasn't working for me anymore. I didn't realise that creating a new foundation meant I had to relearn so much about myself that I didn't know. I wish I had known it all earlier in life so I could have gained my freedom so much sooner! But I am so grateful that I saw it and had time to recreate it all over again, better than I ever thought possible.

Through learning, recognising signs and sheer determination I can see how much more in control I am of my emotions and my life. I appreciate how powerful my free will is and how I can use it to achieve what truly makes me happy, because my happiness does matter. I slowly worked through the pain by giving myself all I needed; self-love, trust, faith, compassion, hope, positive affirmations and belief in myself that I have never had before. The most important thing I gave myself was freedom. Freedom from all I was, to now being free to be who I want to be, and *I am* free. It helped me find my own magnificence!

There are some stages in life where we are challenged in some way and they stand out and are recognised. Some of these are; 'The Rebellious Teenager', 'The Hormonal Pregnant Woman', 'The Empty Nester', 'The Retired Workaholic' and the 'Midlife Crisis'. The teenager is when the child is changing from this little person that saw life in a simple way and then they see life with expectations, more responsibility and change. Hormones are flowing and they don't know themselves anymore. Their needs and wants change and they don't understand all the emotions that are happening inside them. Some become rebellious and push all the limits, others isolate themselves because it's safer that way. It is usually a time when parents are also forced to change again as they can't stop the changes that are occurring around them.

Then there is the Hormonal Pregnant Woman and her constantly changing body and life. She is consumed with fear of something going wrong and her failure to take care of this love that is growing inside her. She is consumed by a protectiveness she had never felt before whilst she nurtures her growing unborn baby in her belly. Her body is being stretched, organs squashed and a tiredness sweeps over her as her body focuses on nurturing this new life. She questions her relationship, other parents' actions, flies off the handle over the smallest things, all because she is thrown into change and she is scared. It will never just be her anymore. The free spirited girl is gone, and now she is a mother – massive yet precious change.

The Empty Nester, the parent who has given their all to their children and family. It's where they felt needed and wanted. When the children grow up and leave home it causes a crisis for this parent. They don't know what to do with themselves – the feeling of 'I don't know who I am'. They have spent many years making sure everyone else had what they wanted and forgot themselves. I was blessed to understand this level, and when my last child left home, I knew who I was. I was able to celebrate what I'd achieved by being a mother. I helped them grow up to be good humans, and I hadn't lost them, they were only mine on loan. Now I've gained their partners and a gorgeous grandson, and the family grows.

The Retired Workaholic stumbles if they are a robot. They had a routine, got up, went to work, worked hard and came home. They were at work more than they were at home or with their family, their tribe. Retirement feels boring because they feel they have nothing to get up for. Not everyone loves retirement. The robot can spiral into the basement if they find they have an empty life, as they had forgotten to nurture those around them as well as themselves. If their partner isn't in what is known as the Robot level, they can drag them on holidays, caravanning, anything to keep them busy, but in time the Robot feelings are still there. They will hopefully find a hobby they can immerse themselves in that they actually enjoy, and therefore break the cycle. Otherwise, they will sit in an armchair and wonder where their life has gone.

Then you have the Midlife Crisis. This is seen as the rebellious adult but how I see it is, you get to an age and you realise how totally lost you are. You haven't lived the life you had envisioned for yourself and you want to grab it before it's too late. You feel life is getting shorter and you don't have a lot of time left. You feel tired of being the robot, you've lost yourself, you are going through the motions in life and you've had enough! That awakening is like a jolt to the system. You may be going through a loss of some kind, be it relationship, job or even sense of self. Some go crazy during this time, but if you understood yourself better, you wouldn't have to go through such a harrowing shift in one big jolt. Being true to yourself earlier and making small adjustments could take you towards what you really want for yourself with more understanding and ease. Your dreams do matter.

I use the analogy of how we are on our path, and someone or something takes us off track by pulling our arm to where they want you to go and all of a sudden you find yourself somewhere you don't want to be. Your course has changed. You may feel so lost that you can't find your way back onto your own path. You then spend a lot of time either being anxious and stressed over finding your way back on track, or you procrastinate because you are totally off track of where you want to go. So, you go nowhere because you give up. It can take years if you choose to stay in that 'lost' way of thinking, but really all you have to do is focus on the path again and you're there. It's an intention, a decision you make that shifts your perception, and you bring forward change. You get back on course, put your life back into your own hands and move forward. No one can change your life without your permission and only you are in control of changing your own life. It is your life after all.

I shall write about universal energy because I am a strong believer in this power. The energy you put out always finds its way back to you. Some call it karmic energy or 'karma'; do something bad, bad comes back; do good, and it finds you too! Some call it Law of Attraction. Same thing in the big scheme of things, but know you are constantly attracting what you give out. This was a powerful lesson for me.

How we 'really' feel about ourselves, attracts that same energy. So if you feel negative about yourself, you will attract situations and people that will validate that feeling you already have. For example, I used to think that my ex-husband made me feel alone, insignificant and not important to him, when in reality I already felt those things about myself, he just showed this to me. I could see the reflection of what I was putting out – and I was getting it back. It was like my ex was standing in front of me, holding a mirror, showing me what I thought about myself.

You can smile and be a robot, but your true energy is always reflected out. No matter how much you pretend to smile so others think you are okay, your insides tell a different story, and this radiates in your energy surrounding you. That's why when you are hiding behind a smile, someone that is in tune with you will always ask, 'Are you okay?' Feeling good on the inside about who you are reflects back on you in relationships, opportunities, situations – anything that holds energy. If you visit someone with a dog and you are unwell, sad or lonely, you will find the dog comes to sit near you, it knows. Your energy speaks volumes.

Realise this and you are on the road to changing your life and aligning with your path again and attracting what you do want for yourself.

If you feel life is against you, now is the time to take control, make changes and discover the levels of awareness that will help you move through life freely. Life isn't against you; Life is just waiting for you to live it. Your happiness is an inside job! Your job! Remember that all you need is a DREAM. BELIEVE in that dream. TRUST in who you are. Allow yourself to EVOLVE and BECOME the you that you have always wanted to be.

Chapter 2

THE FIVE LEVELS OF AWARENESS

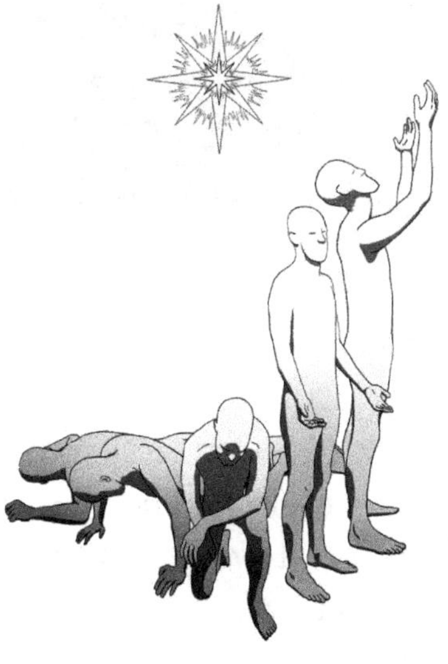

There are five levels of awareness to recognise, understand and work with.

See it like an apartment building and this building is your emotional self.

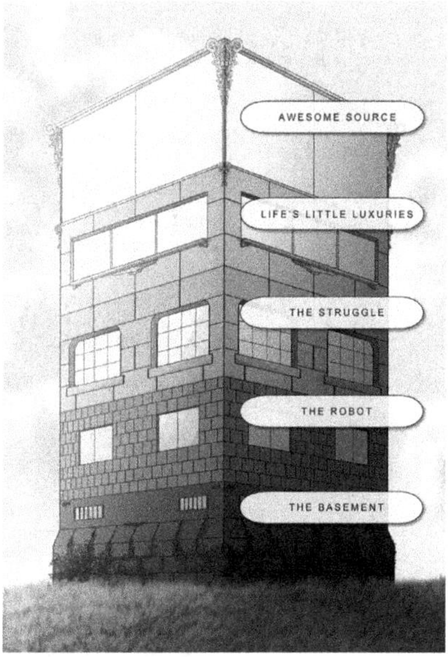

The five levels from the bottom up are:

1. THE BASEMENT – Connection to Self
2. THE ROBOT (Level 1) – The Merry-go-round
3. THE STRUGGLE (Level 2) – Breaking Barriers
4. LIFE'S LITTLE LUXURIES (Level 3) – Appreciation & Gratitude
5. AWESOME SOURCE – The Penthouse – Universal Connection

The foundation of your building is based on your belief and awareness of yourself. The strength of your belief and awareness, the stronger the foundation and sturdier the building. What you deeply believe about yourself and what your inner voice tells you can either weaken or strengthen this foundation that you build your existence on. This can come from actions, words or views of the past. If you have a poor belief system from your childhood or adulthood, your awareness may be built on these emotions, giving you negative uneven ground and your building may look like the Leaning Tower of Pisa. Our foundation is such an important part as this is the ground we walk on in our everyday lives. When the foundation is weak, it struggles to hold on to the life you are creating and can break, letting your world come crashing down. But if you choose to build a solid foundation based on a strong life focus, your foundation will support you and hold you firmly. As you develop and evolve through the levels, you are reinforcing the foundation. By healing any vulnerable weaknesses in this ground, you are strengthening this foundation to then withstand any earthquake, any attack...you can then withstand anything that is thrown at you!

LIFE is the ELEVATOR that moves you through each level. Life can and will throw many unexpected curve balls at you, which will take you through different emotions and can take you through the different levels. Of course, in life, we all want to live in the penthouse where there is a sense of peace, comfort and you feel happy with all around you, but life can be unpredictable and fragile at times. Precious moments in life can only be truly seen when we are placed in difficult situations, and we are pushed to limits we never knew possible. So instead of going to the penthouse, you may end up in level two or even dropped into the Basement. Always remember, it's not the destination but the journey you will travel to find who you really are and what you are capable of.

We either aspire to live in the penthouse, or we fear the thought of being stuck in the Basement and try to avoid its existence totally! Everything in the middle seems to be ignored like it doesn't exist. Happy – sad, light – dark, penthouse – Basement. But there are so many shades in between to be appreciated! Just having an understanding of these levels will be your compass in life and will help you accept where you are and how to work your way through it. The journey is yours to take, and only you can decide how you move within these levels. Your life is in your hands, and you are always in control of how you react to it. You're powerful, more than you realise. Understanding the levels will help you gain control and guide you through life with more ease and less resistance.

The Five Levels Explained

No matter who you are; your culture, religion, financial status, colour, gender, language or your age, you will visit these Five Levels of Awareness at some point in your life! You are human after all, and this is life.

The Basement is our opportunity for connection to self. It's seen as the bottom, where everything feels hopeless, life feels cruel, cold, and it's where we feel alone. I call this depression, sadness, despair, loneliness, abandonment – where you are isolating yourself and needing to shut everything out. As you become more aware, this level becomes your constructive time alone, your time out and self-care time. This place isn't always doom and gloom, it actually has a beautiful side to it. When you see this level for what it truly is, your life can really change from the ground up! All you need is a dream.

The Robot level is what I like to call the merry-go-round. Society can get stuck in this phase. Walking around doing what you have to do like a robot. You get told what is expected of you and you do it with no thought of what you want or feel. It's that level of mere existence with no vision or goal. Sometimes you don't see you are in this phase until you wake up maybe years later and wonder where your life has gone. You just keep going around and around attracting the same lessons – but still not learning – until you decide to get off and change. Believe in your dream.

The Struggle is the time of breaking barriers that you have set around yourself. It's when you wake up and realise you want more in your life. You have a dream but you don't believe that you can attain it, but you still want it. You do have an inner spark, a passion, an inner desire of wanting something different, something better for yourself, but you battle the inner critic that keeps you questioning yourself. You just don't want to be stuck anymore! You see a dream but feel hopeless to get there, but you just want to try. This phase is the biggest in life and presents the biggest opportunity if your desire is strong enough to make changes. Trust in who you are and where you want to be.

Life's Little Luxuries is where you feel appreciation and gratitude. You begin finding self-belief, and the universe responds and starts to give you little 'aha' moments that you allow yourself to enjoy. Those are the little moments when you feel life is good and something is going right for you for a change. We have these moments all the time as life blesses us with little gifts but if we are in the darker levels these can be missed, unseen or even not appreciated. These can even be the things we take for granted, like a sunrise and a hot shower. When you recognise them, they can really open you up to receiving so many more blessings into your life. It's about putting on your rose-coloured glasses and smiling. Allow yourself to evolve.

Awesome Source is that realisation where you know that you and the universe are connected. It's when life flows and it all makes sense! It's when you know why you are here and what your purpose is. Opportunities present themselves and doors open. Life is awesome! This is when what you have desired or asked for is delivered. This is the place where you align with the universe and you work in sync, so your words are being heard and what you need seems to find its way to you. You can really feel the happiness in your life because you and the universe are aligned. This is the place of happiness and joy. The elixir of life. Connected to that awesome source of energy, you become the you that you have always wanted to be.

Movement Within The Five Levels

As you take the journey of self-discovery, you will learn about the levels, their high and low points and how to navigate through them. You will recognise the feelings of being in each level and know how to work within this space so that challenges are worked through to help you and not block you.

As opportunities to change arise, the elevator of life will take you through these levels, either up or down, depending on your lessons and growth. When you understand each level, you will have insight on how to move without resistance, as resistance makes the process longer. For example, the longer you tell yourself that you can't get out of the Basement, the longer you will stay in there.

You will probably find that you spend a majority of time in the bottom three levels of awareness. As you learn to trust and gain self-confidence in yourself and your dream, you will gravitate towards the top levels, where you will feel gratitude and connected to your inner self. It's always up to you how long this takes because this is your life, and you do it your way. As I said, resistance slows the process. You have to be willing to change and take steps towards wanting a more fulfilling life for yourself and the opportunities you desire.

It has taken me a couple of years to consciously change from living in the bottom three levels (Basement, Robot & Struggle) with a glimpse of the top two (Life's Luxuries and Awesome Source). My past beliefs were like hooks in my back stopping me from moving forward freely, but in time, I lovingly removed those hooks, changed my belief system and now I enjoy living in the top three levels (Struggle, Life's Little Luxuries, Awesome Source), with glimpses of the bottom two (Basement & Robot). As I understood the process, of how my fear and resistance to change held me back, I made sure I limited my time in the lower levels by letting the emotions in, acknowledging them, feeling them and then letting them go. As I stopped fighting against where I was, the time I was there became shorter and shorter. My time in the Basement became constructive instead of destructive. When I now find myself in the Basement or Robot phase, I know that life is giving me an opportunity to learn and grow as a person in the form of a challenge. Just knowing that helps me let go of all the negative words from my inner critic. I don't empower my inner critic to allow fear to defeat my progress. I acknowledge it, learn why I'm feeling the fear, and let it go so I can do what I need, to rise to the challenge.

The bottom three levels are heavy and keep us down if they take control. It feels hard to push through to the top levels when you feel down, but in time, as you understand where you are, you can put in place what you need to do and learn the lessons that these levels are offering you. You are *always* the captain of your ship, and *you are* in control. Don't let that fear hold you down. Befriend it and keep moving.

You see, it's all a journey with no destination apart from living the life you want, with no regrets, no guilt and being empowered with self-love. Once you love yourself, others will love you and you will love them, no expectations, no conditions, just pure love. You will love all aspects of them, even their shortcomings as love sees pain differently. Love sees the challenges others have too and instead of feeling anger, hatred or jealousy, love heals all. It's when you understand and trust the process of life and you feel and accept your emotions and honour them.

When you know you are a part of everything and everything is a part of you, this is when you and the universe align.

When you understand the Five Levels of Awareness, you can embrace them, knowing that they are natural places to be in and you can navigate through them so much easier.

You begin to let go of the path of self-doubt, and you travel on the path of self-love with an open mind and a stronger foundation.

Remember that all you need is a DREAM. BELIEVE in that dream. TRUST in who you are. Allow yourself to EVOLVE and BECOME the you that you have always wanted to be.

Typical Language of the Five Levels

Level	Language Used
THE BASEMENT	I don't want to be an adult anymore! I hate my life. I'm done, done with life. Leave me alone. I don't see the point of why I'm even here. I want to curl up in a little ball and I don't want to come out.
THE ROBOT	I have to do this! I have no choice. Nothing changes. I'm going nowhere. I don't know what I want. Why am I here? What's the point?
THE STRUGGLE	I want change! I can't keep doing this anymore! I want more for myself. I know what I want but can I have it? Am I good enough? Am I worth it?
LIFE'S LITTLE LUXURIES	That was fun! I have to do that again. That's so beautiful, it took my breath away. I am so grateful. What a great opportunity.
AWESOME SOURCE	I am so blessed. I love my life. Everything is falling into place. I am exactly where I'm meant to be. I am connected.

Chapter 3

THE BASEMENT

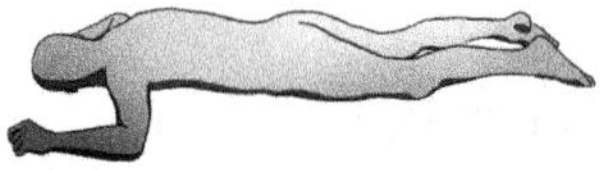

The Basement is the place where you come face to face with your nightmares, yet it becomes the place where you will learn the most about yourself. The Basement can be your darkness yet can become your light.

The Basement is the lowest point in life where you feel alone, isolated or in a crisis. When everything seems to feel like it's going wrong in your life. There are days you don't want to get up. You don't want to shower, face others or interact in any form with anyone. It can be a lonely, gut wrenching and isolating place to find yourself. It's where you say, 'I don't care anymore, is life worth living?' It's where suicides may take place, ending an incredible life and stealing the possibilities that life had to offer.

BUT THE BASEMENT IS NOT YOUR ENEMY!!

Let me tell you now, you can and will visit the Basement in your lifetime. It is important that you understand, the Basement is *not* there to take anything from you, but to give to you.

I first experienced the Basement as a child because of abuse at the hand of a family member. I felt overwhelmed with fear and did not understand what was happening to me. Many times, the Basement has called me into its depth of despair in my lifetime, and it took me to my lowest point. Many times I almost lost myself. I had to feel the despair and the darkness that came with it to fully understand it. Without all I had learned about these levels, I would probably not be here to write this book and tell you my story.

The last time I found myself in the Basement, my marriage had ended the year before and I was still grieving the loss and finding it very difficult to let go. I knew it was over and there was no turning back. It left me completely gutted and hollow. I was about to lose my home because I couldn't make the mortgage repayments on my own, and my injuries from a previous accident prevented me from working. The house needed work and I was trying to sell it, but I barely had the basic funds to live day to day. My best friend had just passed away after a long battle with cancer. I missed her terribly and I just couldn't see anything good in my life. I had lost control. I felt helpless and broken. I sat there and thought that everyone would be better off if I wasn't here. I thought my life insurance would pay the mortgage and the kids would be okay, as they were now married and had their own lives. I wasn't needed anymore and my job was done as a mother. Negativity was taking over and the words were loud in my head telling me I was unlovable, useless, a burden on everyone and a total failure. No matter how many wonderful things surrounded my life, I just couldn't see them. I was drowning in my own misery. I would go to sleep crying, wake up in the middle of the night in total despair and panic. When I woke in the morning I felt inconsolable that I had to do it all over again. I woke up one day and wrote a letter to say goodbye to my loved ones. I explained how sorry I was that I couldn't find a way to fix things, and that in time they would be okay. I cleaned the house and I found a location where I would take myself as my last place. I got in my car and cried for a while as I felt it was the last time I would be leaving my home. I was crying for all I felt I'd lost, what a failure I was and how worthless I felt. As I started to drive, in amongst the fear of what I was about to do and the heartbreaking sadness, came the warm feeling of love that was inside me. I felt the love I had for my beautiful grandson and how I would miss his smile and his cuddles. I felt the love of my two children who I would miss terribly as their love was ingrained in my soul. The love was so powerful that I had the realisation I really didn't want to do this. I didn't want to die, but I felt overwhelmed by the thought of not having another choice. The feeling was so gut-wrenching and so painful. At that moment I knew I needed help so the most courageous thing I could do for myself was to drive to my doctor and ask for the help I needed. Within hours I was sitting with my counsellor. I realised I owed this to the little girl inside me who was hoping I would make great choices and make her dreams come true, because she deserved that. I couldn't just let it end this way.

When my counsellor asked me why I didn't go through with it, my answer was easy; first it was my family, and then my words were, 'I felt bad for the poor bastard that was going to find me and have to deal with that trauma.' My own PTSD (post-traumatic stress disorder) was hard enough to deal with that I simply couldn't do it to someone else. I went on to tell her that I believed if I left any unfinished lessons in this life I would have to come back and do it all again and I didn't want to come back in another life and redo 'this pain' all over again! I cried as I listed off all the other reasons: 'My new grandson would never know me, my children would be lost without me as we are so close, and it would crush my parents, my friends...the list went on and on. I knew I didn't want to die, I just felt like there was no other choice, I felt like I was lying with my face flat to the floor with no energy to get up. But as I spoke to my counsellor I realised there was a choice, there absolutely was. I made that choice in that moment. I chose to live; I chose to have a dream. I chose to do all I could to have that dream.

My dream was to be happy. That's it. 'Happy'. It was enough for now.

Little by little, I put all the tools together and I turned this dark place into a place of opportunity. I found many more reasons to live, and in hindsight, I saw a magnificence and strength in myself I had never seen before. I would have missed so many wonderful moments – all the beautiful times with my family and friends that I have had since. I would have missed a love I thought never possible. Life did get good again, I just had to find myself, and I did. I had to work from the inside out. I had to love and believe in myself in a way I had never done before. I let go of the negative feelings I had about myself one by one and replaced them with love.

We sometimes think that our outside circumstances are the reasons why we feel 'bad' but it's *an inside job*. I always thought my feelings of insignificance, being unloved, not beautiful and not worth fighting for came from my outside circumstances. I thought it was everyone else and the situations I found myself in that were making me feel like that. Sure, other people's actions did bring it out in me, but in reality, it was me. I was the one who felt insignificant to myself, I didn't see myself as important. I didn't love myself because I felt unlovable. I didn't feel beautiful because when I looked in the mirror I wasn't who I wanted to be or how others wanted me to be and I didn't accept who I was. I didn't fight for myself, because I didn't want to upset anyone so I placed myself at the bottom of the list of importance. I didn't trust myself because I didn't believe I had my own best interests at heart, and I had to ask for other peoples' opinions because mine weren't worth listening to. All the circumstances life threw at me made me question who I was, how I felt about myself, and they mirrored the negative because that's how I felt about me. It's heartbreaking what we do to ourselves. When we realise we have been standing in front of a mirror all along, it really is a pivotal moment. It's when you understand, *you are the key*.

Loving and accepting myself became my first hurdle and my first challenge. I had to start from the beginning and rebuild myself piece by piece – the way I wanted, not what others wanted or expected of me, but me...what I wanted to be. Instead of The Basement destroying me, it saved me and gave me a place where I could learn from my past instead of it continuing to pull me back. It was my choice whether I stayed here and continued to let this level teach me or decide to move on.

The Basement is a place that helps you to look at yourself, your life and take stock of what has taken you down here. At first you see it as a negative place because a situation, person or your own inner feelings dumped you down here. However, it's what you do there that is the true gift. This is where you find strength, where you wake up the warrior.

You may be asking, how can such a dark place give you anything good or positive? Sad songs, heartbreaking poetry, emotionally driven movie scripts, amazing novels with stories of sad times and hope – even this book – where do you think these came from? The Basement. Even popular song writers, artists and successful people have hit this bottom, but created something quite amazing whilst they were down here. Those emotions can't just be created, they must be felt with the heart and soul. Every tear, scream, sleepless night, heartfelt destruction teased all those words and emotions out. You can't write it or sing it without feeling this level. When we hear those songs, or watch those movies or read the books, we too feel that pain, sadness and heartbreak as we experience the Basement from someone else's point of view. We see their tears and feel their heartbreak. Many hearts are touched by these emotions, this pain, this heartache because many can relate to it. These artists then create their masterpieces from their experiences. This level is not a place to fear but one that can bring opportunity!

You can and will visit the Basement in your lifetime but it is NOT there to take anything from you. This level holds a lot of power as it can really bring out something great inside of you, and only in hindsight can you see the great strength you had when you were here. Never underestimate yourself, you can make this place the miracle you have been waiting for by just keeping it simple. Focus on the simple things you may take for granted, like being alive and breathing. Now that's worth being grateful for! As long as we are alive, we are here, we are present. It's a start point and simple. Even in the Basement, no matter how helpless things feel, you will have life, breath and you always have the freedom to change what's happening *to* you and in time you will see why it's happening *for* your greater good.

When we find ourselves helpless, all we want to do is close our eyes because we just want things to stop. So if you find yourself in the Basement, if you want to do nothing, then do nothing. If you want to sleep, sleep. If you want to stay in your pyjamas all day, do it! If you want to read, watch movies, play games, whatever it is, do it! This is your time-out place where you can gather yourself. You can choose an hour, half a day or a whole day, but it's important to set a time as the Basement can swallow you up and you can find yourself lost there for a long time. At first, you can do simple things...breathe. Give yourself this time because you deserve it! We live in a negative world where stress, money problems, work pressures, disconnected families and beliefs are being questioned. The Basement makes you stop! It helps you find out what's really going on in your heart and mind. Don't let the universe do this for you! By this I mean, when you need change and you avoid it, fear it, or turn your back to it and continue to live life with tunnel vision, the universe will find a way to force change upon you and take you to the Basement with a thud, such as; engineering the sack from work, a relationship bust-up or a major unexpected change. These events force our hand, because we need to change. So, before the universe brings this change, give yourself the gift of this time out to assess your life. It will give you time to understand your thoughts, feelings and the circumstances that have brought you to this place. This 'quiet time' can be the time you need – to help you get back on track, to delivering the changes you so desperately want. This is the place where your dream is born.

As you take steps to change, sometimes you may feel that you are failing but you are not failing at all. You are learning about yourself and how to give yourself what you need. You are honouring, valuing and gifting yourself the time you deserve. You've done that for others, and you have nothing left to give them because you have left nothing for yourself. Your cup is empty.

When you have a Basement day, see it as releasing the pressure from the pressure cooker before it blows! If all the signs are there for you to take time out and you avoid it, you can get sick, really sick. Burnouts can happen in this place. This can cause health problems which can work against you and in the process you can lose your job, your relationship, and even yourself if you don't give this time to you. You need to fill your own cup.

Some may see the Basement as a failure, so if they go there, they think they have failed in their life, but the Basement is a place of integrity and resilience. It's from the Basement that truly amazing people have come. It's where lessons are learnt and miracles happen. The Basement is a place where you can step away from everything around you, so you are just with 'you'.

When we see the Basement in a negative way, we shut ourselves off because we are wanting to avoid the world, people and existence outside of us. This is the dark side of the Basement.

These are some of the phrases used in this negative side of the Basement.

I hate my life.
I'm done, done with life.
Leave me alone.
I don't see the point of why I'm even here.
I don't want to be here anymore.
I want to curl up into a ball, I don't want to come out.
I want to disappear.
I want to get in the car and drive and never come back.
I am NOT okay.

These are the phrases you use in the depths of despair and you want to be alone. Sometimes there is the absolute need to just be alone and there is nothing wrong with that. We don't always have to be around people. If we allow ourselves to just be, without the guilt, the fear and the criticism, our time in the Basement can be short and sweet instead of long and painful. Instead of fighting to push it away, let it in and understand it. Some see the emotions of the Basement as being weak. Far from it, this isn't a place for the weak. This is a place where miracles happen, where you find the strength to move forward. This is a place of great power if you let it be.

When we say, 'I'll never feel better', or 'This will never get better', we have decided to stay in this level. We have given up. We have made a choice that we don't want things to get better. Remember that when you say, '*I'll never* feel better', you're putting out energy that's limiting your potential, so you will attract more to make you feel worse. 'My life will never change!' Say it enough and it's all you will believe. Instead, if we understood the energy of our words, we would save ourselves a lot of time being in this place, possibly years, because the people who are trying to avoid being in the Basement are the ones who end up living in the Basement for most of their life. All they know is being in this level, and they become too afraid to leave. If you have been in prison long enough, you are too afraid to be free, because you have forgotten what it's like to be free again.

The Basement is the lowest we can feel but I want you to look at this place in a different way, a much more positive way. Sometimes we are afraid of change and letting go because we worry about what's going to happen. The fear of losing someone or something can be so overwhelming that we feel like we are drowning.

When I was in this place, I had dark thoughts swirling around my mind because I had forgotten how to feel happy. I felt like I was never going to feel happy again, and if I couldn't be happy, then what was the point of living? My memories of being happy were so distant and unreachable that I felt overpowered by a feeling of dread and sadness. These dark times manipulated me into believing that nothing good would ever happen to me again. I had lost so much around me, and this was all I could see and feel.

When people asked me how I was, my usual answer was 'fine' or a reluctant 'good', but I was not fine...I was not good. Saying those words just deflected what I didn't want others to see. I didn't want to bother them with my problems, I felt I wasn't worth that attention. I also said those words because if I said it enough, maybe I would believe it. It worked before, maybe it would work again. I did a lot of pretending and acting like I was fine because if people saw how much pain I was in, they would worry, and I didn't want them to do that. I was also afraid they would abandon me and see me as negative and too much hard work. Frankly, I didn't think owning how I really felt was going to help me in any way.

Why are we so afraid to say how we really feel? Are we afraid of being judged weak? But this is like putting a bandage on an open wound. The open wound is bleeding and painful and the bandage can't really hold it together. If it ever heals it will leave a big scar and it will never be the same again.

When I felt the Basement the last time, I knew I didn't want to die but I just didn't want to live like that anymore. Just that realisation was powerful for me. The emotion of love helped me. Hearing the emotion of love in my loved one's voices really helped. The love for those around me meant so much to me. My grandson's beautiful face and his giggle, and my own children's faces etched in my heart and mind. Also deep down I knew I wanted more in this life, and a little voice reminded me that I deserved it.

The dark times creep in so slow you can miss them coming, and when they leave it can be the same way, one day you just feel better.

I sought professional help because I knew I couldn't do it on my own. Just saying, 'I need help' and receiving that help made me feel safe in knowing that someone knew how I really felt and could help me. But I also knew that without me, their words and help would amount to nothing because I had to want this for myself and take their assistance with open arms. The tools they provided me with at the time were all that I needed to move towards the change I so desperately wanted. I was the key factor, I had to want to grow from this and not stay where I was.

It was a moment by moment, day by day process. Some days it was like I was treading water and my legs were getting tired, but I couldn't give up on myself anymore. I started to do more of what helped me; I would go to the beach and get some fresh air. Feeling the sunshine and breeze on my face cleared the cobwebs I felt were surrounding me. Listening to the water, putting my feet in and letting go as I cried was all therapeutic for me. There was a sense of calmness inside me that I hadn't felt for such a long time.

It wasn't until a couple of months after the changes had occurred that I looked back and saw how far I'd taken myself. I felt proud in how I had dealt with such a place that almost cost me my life. Every cherished moment I would say to myself, I would have missed such a precious blessing. And if I have a moment of feeling alone or hopeless, I remind myself of how strong I am to have seen and felt that darkness and survived it. I see how far I've come, and I know I don't want to die, I want to live my best life where I am free and happy.

It was at this point I felt I was ready to come out of the dark and feel the sunlight on my face again. The Basement served me well. It gave me courage to step forward.

You see, it's in the Basement where we fight our demons and come in touch with our true selves, our true feelings, and the only way is up. The Basement is where you find self-acceptance, the will to carry on, and where you see the strength and power you hold. The Basement is a connection back to your soul.

There are times *I choose* to visit the Basement. I have what I call, Basement days. On those days I choose to nurture myself instead of torture myself. I know that if I'm sometimes challenged by life and those old feelings start to be stirred, instead of growing that seed of doubt and becoming exhausted from over thinking, I know it's time to give myself some 'me' time. I schedule a morning or a day in my diary to focus on me. The Basement has changed from a place I was afraid of and didn't want to visit, to a place of rest, renewal and meditation. Scheduling this time in my diary meant that my mind, body and soul needed this time to self-care, self-evaluate and give back to myself. Whether I watch a movie, sleep, cry, whatever I do, it's going to be ME time. For some, 'me' time can be seen as selfish, but it is actually 'self-care', and that is so important to give to yourself. If someone is down, you care for them, so why is it so wrong to care for you? I take this time out if I've got a lot of things on my mind and I am feeling down and I need to cry. I give myself this time because I need to understand my emotions so I can acknowledge how I am really feeling about things, and it's okay! Just like I make time for others, I too need to make time for myself. My job involves helping others most of the time, so I honour myself by giving myself the time I need. I give myself what I need to help me.

Some typical Basement days may include little things like:

1. **Wake up with no alarm.** Waking up on your own when your body has had enough sleep.
2. **Lying in bed** for a little while after you've woken and just breathe. Be aware of the sound of your breath as you breathe in and out. This will help you quieten your mind. You deserve peace in your mind. In the past I would wake up and the panic would begin, the feeling of helplessness would flood in and it would consume me, and I found scheduling this time to just 'be' was about nurturing the self. This quiet time is a good form of meditation, so if you have some music, use it to help you quieten your mind.

3. **I love pyjama days!** Sometimes on my Basement day, I love being in them as they're a symbol that it's caring-for-me day. On this day I will either read, write, watch something I have been wanting to watch on TV or a movie that uplifts me. Sometimes I bake. Do whatever you want to do that gives you quiet head space.
4. **Get outdoors!** A walk or a drive with the window down and music playing. One of my favourite things to do is to get in my car, take a drink and something to do, and park under a tree with the view of the ocean at my favourite part of the beach. Something about the ocean relaxes me, helps me stop and energises me. I see this as a gift I give myself.Even 15 minutes in nature is enough to have a positive effect, both mentally and physically. It's been proven to boost your serotonin levels, which changes your mood. Whilst outside, go for a walk, water and talk to the plants. You can make this a routine, first thing in the morning, or before you pick the kids up from school or even at sunset. A time that works for you.On those days when you aren't feeling physical and want to be alone to process thoughts, you could even park at your favourite place with the window down. Feeling that beautiful breeze or even the sunshine on your face. Feel that energy touch you. Nature has a way of getting into your soul.

Don't fight off the Basement time, embrace it. It's a time of self-care and self-love. This time allows you to grow and understand how you work, and to find what works for you.

Find what relaxes you, or a place you can go that helps you breathe easier and frees you from whatever constraints you have in your life.

Let those chains go right now. Make the decision today to listen to yourself, nurture and love yourself and not be afraid to take that big step to do it.

We live in a busy world where the symptoms of depression, stress and anxiety are rising, so no matter what is happening in your life, you need to make the time to schedule this Basement time for you. It doesn't matter how long this time is. It could be a Basement hour, half day, full day. Put it in your calendar or diary when you start to feel the pressure is building. Don't wait until you can't take it anymore or when it's overwhelming as you risk getting into the dark part of the Basement. If you listen to yourself, you will know when you need this time.

I was given a vision about this level. I was shown a seed nestled in the dirt in the dark. The uncertainty of whether it would sprout occupied my thoughts, but if the seed is given the right conditions it will blossom into the mightiest of trees.

So in this level you have three choices;

1. You can drop to the dark side of this level and give up or totally break down.
2. You can stay in this place and reap the benefits of what this level alone can offer you.
   Or
3. You can make that choice to gather yourself and step out of here.

The choice is always yours to make.

I suggest you take the step and make the change today.

Remember I am here with you along the way, you are never alone.

Let me be the voice inside you that says, 'I believe in you.'

Take my hand, let's take the next step in your journey together.

All you need is a DREAM.

Chapter 4

HELP YOURSELF WHEN IN THE BASEMENT

EAT PROPERLY

What we eat really has a significant effect on our body and mind. It's okay sometimes to have something that is unhealthy – after all we are human – but make sure you are having nutritional food to help your body and mind work for you and not against you.

I've always been a great vegetable and salad eater, but I have always loved my carbs. I had to narrow these down as my 'sometimes' food, as I understood this particular group was what I'd 'emotionally eat'. I lacked protein and legumes, and since eating more of these foods, my brain seems to be sharper. Find those foods for you and have more of them. Our bodies always talk to us and I listen to my body a lot more than I ever have. If your body doesn't like something and it tells you, listen. As I've grown older, my body doesn't like some types of dairy products and meats. I just take note and try to avoid them.

GET ENOUGH SLEEP!

It's a well-known fact that when we don't get enough sleep, our mood and energy level is lowered, and that is just after one bad night's sleep. If you do that night after night, week after week, it affects your ability to deal with challenges and to see things clearly. With a foggy tired mind everything seems much more difficult than it actually is. Not having good quality sleep can affect our physical, mental, emotional and spiritual self, which in turn weighs us down with negative side effects, such as depression, anxiety, stress, weight gain and much more.

Try to have a sleep routine of going to bed and waking up around the same time. My sleep used to be shocking! When I was in the Basement, I found myself not being able to sleep. I'd go to bed in the early hours of the morning and sleep half the morning away. That only made me more detached, more down. I then started to go to bed earlier, at the same time every night. I would wake up clearer in my mind and be able to get what I needed to get done before lunchtime. Mentally, I felt so much more productive and healthier in my mind and it made me feel good to get so much more done in a day.

CONNECT WITH YOUR TRIBE

This helps you feel connected and allows you to be a part of something more than yourself. It gives you family, friends and community. Being detached only isolates you more. I have learnt as an introvert that there is value in me being social and spending time with my family, friends and my community because it helps me to feel a sense of belonging.

Sometimes sharing how you feel gets it out of your mind and into an open pool where it can be cleansed and nurtured. People can't love and nurture you if you are closed off from them. It's okay to go through some things on your own, as the seed that sprouts does, but sometimes we need shelter and water from others so that we feel cared for. When someone cares, it fills our cup – give someone the chance to fill your cup. Whether you're an introvert or not, your tribe will accept and love you just as you are. They will know your quirks and how you tick, if you are open and honest with them. Be transparent so they know the real you.

In the Basement you may feel out of touch with those around you, maybe this is the opportunity to reconnect. A phone call, a text, or even a chat over a cup of tea. It's been proven that those who are connected to their tribe are much happier and end up living longer. Perfect reason to connect!

MEDITATE

I remember being told years ago to try this, and when I did, I couldn't do it no matter how hard I tried. But I persisted. I tried it in groups but I felt my fear of falling asleep and snoring was so big that I simply wouldn't allow myself the opportunity to just let go. I actually made it harder for myself.

After a few weeks going to a meditation class, knowing fully that I would have to wait 30 minutes for the meditation to finish, I let go and did my very first meditation! And I didn't snore!

In that moment I realised meditation was about letting go. I would lay on my bed, or sit in my car by the beach, even sit in my 'angel room' at home with either soft music or just listening to the sound of my breath. Whether it was five minutes or half an hour, it didn't matter. The more I did this, the better I got at it.

We seem to make meditation complicated, but it really is simple. You can be anywhere, and it can be at any time. Sometimes, I find driving a meditation as I stop thinking about work and worries and focus on the road, like focusing on breathing. Some find themselves in the zone when they exercise.

Create a habit to gift yourself a few minutes every day to listen to your breath in and out. Feeling it fill your lungs and then leaving your body only to come back in is so therapeutic – it helps you focus on the present, not on what was or what will be but now, this moment.

You can try a guided meditation, some music you like to relax to or even silence, whatever makes you happy. Meditation helps your mind have a break. Your brain will thank you for it when it's rested and you can think more clearly. There are lots of positive benefits to meditation, try it today!

TO SHARE, OR NOT TO SHARE, THAT IS THE QUESTION

Sometimes I will share my Basement day with someone I know because I don't want to be alone. It can be sitting with an old friend having a coffee and laughing. Basement days are your choice! You can keep them to yourself or share them. I find for people who are on their own a lot, work at home alone, or live alone, Basement days can offer the choice of bringing someone else into your space, someone who lights up your life in some way. Sometimes, I share my Basement days because in my line of work I can sometimes find myself isolated at home, so going out with a friend for a cup of tea and a chat is just what I need.

TECHNOLOGY DETOX!

Having a break from technology is a healthy practice when you are in the Basement. When I was in Ubud on Nyepi Day, it was 24 hours free of all technology. No phones, internet or TV where I was staying. Initially, I rolled my eyes but by the end of it, my head was relaxed, my eyes clear and I had clarity in what I was doing. There is nothing wrong with logging off from time to time.

I noticed that having time off from technology helped me focus on my goals. I worked with pen and paper again. Planned things out instead of getting sidetracked on social media.

The internet is full of negativity so you can do with a break from that and reclaim your time. Go back to doing something without technology. Get a book out; I love doing crosswords and puzzles. I love connecting with my friends face to face, instead of social media. Have a real conversation. Play cards, or a board game. There are so many things we can do without technology.

Disconnecting, will help you come back into your own life clearer, more focused, and if you don't have a dream, technology may have been masking it. Get some paper and pencils out! There could be an artist or writer in you trying to get out!

WHEN TO GET HELP

If the Basement takes you to a dark place where you feel suicidal or makes you consider self-harm, please take yourself to a place where they offer help. Your doctor's rooms, counsellor, hospital, friend's home, church, anywhere a hand of help is there for you. Don't just ask for help, emphasise the importance of what you need by honestly speaking your truth. Your inner child with his/her dreams pleads with you to take this step. There is always a solution, always. Let love guide you.

When I went to my doctor's rooms to ask for help and I was told my doctor had no appointments for a week, I told them that if I leave, I might hurt myself. The help came instantly. Speak your truth. If you need the help, demand it! It's your right.

BASEMENT AFFIRMATION EXERCISE

Say these affirmations out loud. Emphasise the words most important to you.

I have a dream, and I will make it happen.
I love and respect myself.
I give myself permission to have this time to breathe.
I cherish this life that I have been given.
I am worthy, strong and empowered.
I am the captain of my ship; the writer of my story.

When you finish saying these affirmations, I want you to close your eyes and with each big breath in say or visualise what you want to bring into your life, and with each breath out say or visualise what you are letting go of.

Some examples:

The Basement Affirmations

Breathe in	***Breathe out***
I bring joy into my life	I let go of negativity
I bring love into my life	I let go of fear
I make my dreams happen	I let go of doubt
I am at peace in my world	I let go of anger

Use this Basement time as an opportunity to get to really know yourself and evaluate your life. See the lessons you are facing and connect to what feels right for you. If it means not doing anything at this time, then give it time so you can see it with clarity, and then you will know how to work through it. Remember, sometimes the lessons aren't clear but know that in time you will see them and you will then know what to do.

YOUR BASEMENT JOURNAL

Write a time when you were in the Basement, how you felt and what you had to change to move out of it. Were you resisting change or was change brought to you? This is your space to share your own journey.

Chapter 5

THE ROBOT

This can be a difficult chapter to read as it reflects the characteristics of the Robot level. The Robot is repetitive and confused yet it's a sanctuary that gets you through a part of your life where you are only functioning robotically.

Do you ever feel that life goes past so fast that you wonder where a week, a month or even a year have gone? Maybe you feel like you're just existing or you are totally oblivious to what is going on around you. You feel like you're stuck on a merry-go-round that is going nowhere and feel like you can't get off. Days feel the same, with no direction, you feel like you have lost yourself and your purpose. These are some of the symptoms of living in the Robot level.

You get up, go to work, shower, eat, sleep, and do it all again the next day, sometimes even forgetting what day it is. You may have a family to support, bills to pay, a life that you feel a slave to, a job that you hate or a relationship where you feel like you're living with a stranger. Life can feel like a robotic existence as you go around this vicious circle doing what you need to do with no passion, no joy, no love, a path to nowhere. Sure, you could have a roof over your head, a family that has what they need, you could at least have a job, and you may not be alone, but if you voiced your feelings and/or made any changes it could potentially ruin everything. Whether you're happy or not, you keep doing what's needed and expected of you, but you may feel like you're not living the life you really want, merely existing.

When you start this process, it feels okay for a while, you seem to be doing what you need to do with a purpose in mind. Over time as you wait to get what it is that you want – and there are setbacks and disappointments – you seem to lose track on the path and you begin to doubt your initial purpose. You start feeling overwhelmed in your mind with the inner critic clouding your thoughts. You may feel overwhelmed at times and have too many decisions to make, when not doing anything feels easier than having to decide. You settle. You could be doing this for months, even years without knowing. This is the trait of the 'destructive' Robot.

I've heard some say, 'If I can just work hard at this job that I don't like for six months and get my debt under control, then I can go get the job I really want and I will be okay'. But a year later you are still doing the job you don't like and the debt isn't any less. Changing this situation feels impossible. What if you can't get another job? So, you decide to become a slave to the job you don't like and accept where you are because the original idea is not possible. You feel you have no other option, so it's best to stay where you are. You chose to exist in this job you don't like because you are unwilling to change your situation and you settle for something you don't even want.

As a robot, you do what you have to do and what's expected of you. You may feel there is no choice, no easy option, because at this level everything feels too hard to do. You feel the pressure of others depending on you and you can't let them down, so you put yourself last to make sure what has to be done is done. You make sure everyone else's needs are met and that they are happy, without thinking of your needs and your wants. Your needs are placed at the bottom of a long list of things that you never seem to complete, so your own needs are never reached. This isn't being selfless – over time it will be soul destroying. This isn't life, it's existing!

Doing things robotically, only creates restrictions, limitations and no room for enjoyment. For example, when we are thankful for what we have in this level, it's usually due to fear. Some of these are: Thank God I have this job or how could I keep up with all this debt! Happy wife, happy life. If I give her everything she wants, she won't leave me because she will need me. If I keep the house clean, kids quiet, he will be happy to come home and not find someone younger or better. My husband is busy, my children have their own lives, and I just make sure they all have what they need but I feel lost and empty...I shouldn't complain. If I make any changes, it will affect them so I'd better not.

I hear a lot of these kind of statements in my work.

We give up a lot in the Robot because we are doing what we have to and not what we want to. Dreams may feel distant and unreachable.

- Not enough money to do what you really want to do, so why bother dreaming.
- You feel like you don't deserve your dreams; it only happens for others.
- You give up on the holiday you've always wanted to go on, the car you've always dreamed of driving, even applying for the job you always wanted.
- You don't take chances or risks when opportunities present themselves. You say 'no' even if every part of you wants to say 'yes'.
- You make up excuses of how you can't afford what you want – there's always something you need the money for that's more important.
- You convince yourself that people like you don't get the things they want.
- You hate your job that you're not fulfilled by, but at least you have a job.

- You're in a relationship where you feel empty and lonely, but it's better than being alone.
- You wake up feeling like you don't even know who you are anymore, but you must work, take care of the children – you have responsibilities and your dreams don't matter.
- You feel lifeless, and there is no point in being frustrated because you don't think anything will ever change.
- You feel overwhelmed with choices and decisions you avoid making, and the more you avoid them, the more helpless you feel.

So, you settle on surviving as a robot, so you don't have to aspire or take any steps toward change. You settle because, anything is better than nothing. You accept this as your reason to stay where you are.

Living your life as a robot crushes the essence of the dreamer in you. The Robot level de-sensitises you to excitement and joy, it dampens hope, puts your dreams into a box and tucks it away with a big belief label on it saying, UNATTAINABLE. When you are in this level, you think it's not worth the Struggle to change, you can't see Life's Little Luxuries, you don't think Awesome Source moments are even possible for you and you fight to stay out of the Basement. As the Robot is so close to the Basement, it's easy to drop into it. If the Robot phase goes on too long, the Basement is inevitable.

Your inner critic with its negative self-talk, self-doubt, fear and the lies we tell ourselves to stop us from taking chances, are just some symptoms of the Robot level. The

Robot level disillusions you into thinking you don't know what to do in your life, it clouds your vision, so it gives you the illusion of being stuck. All you want is unachievable.

You can even be blinded at the thought of being in the Robot level, you may not know or see that you are in this place at all. It's one of the most common frames of mind in our busy world because we're not happy with where we are, but we can't be bothered to change. We become complacent with life and give in to the fear of change, so making no changes means no loss. We waste our lives just existing with no purpose. You commonly hear phrases such as, I can't; I am so tired; Is this right? I'm so confused; I don't know what I want; I am so stressed; Should I? What if? I'm so busy.

The Destructive Robot

Being a destructive robot can look like this: you may have been neglecting your health, your relationship, your finances, your inner voice...you may not realise you have been in the Robot level until your whole world comes crashing down. This can be:

Your Relationship – You could be just existing in a relationship, blinded by your partners unhappiness or even your own. Then one day you hear or say these words, 'I can't do this anymore'. If you are in the Robot level on the receiving end, you won't have even seen this coming. You are in shock and don't know what happened, where did it go wrong? If you said it, then you realised you just couldn't keep going around in circles anymore.

This can even occur in relationships with those close to you – parents, siblings, children, family and friends. You miss the signs that one of the children may need you, they may need to be heard or just might need your hug. You are so robotic in your own life that you have missed birthdays, celebrations, illnesses – even the death of someone significant. As a robot you do what you have to do but you're not fully present in the emotional moments.

I have heard many people talk about regrets as they have gotten older. Most of them regret time, and what they could have done with it. One of the saddest things I heard was a hard-working mother in her 60s who was telling me about her son and the distance between them. 'I didn't realise he needed me and now he is grown up and doesn't need me anymore.' Observe those close to you. Don't let the Robot level steal these moments from you.

YOUR WORK

You could be in a robotic job, doing the same thing over and over again. No job enjoyment or satisfaction. You don't get the promotion, you don't even try. You don't feel worthy of better; you either do more than expected or can't be bothered giving anything to it; you receive no recognition and it continues to dishearten you, but you do it, fooling yourself to think you won't find better; or you may not like your job at all, but it gives you money and that's all that matters until one day you get sick or you are made redundant. Then you realise that all you worked hard towards has collapsed and you were just a number. Or you could quite possibly stay in this job for the rest of your working life, at the end holding on to regret of never branching out to do what you really wanted to do.

YOUR HEALTH

You may not sleep enough, eat properly, drink enough water, drink too much alcohol, smoke, take drugs/medication, are not physically active, even isolate yourself indoors and create an unhealthy vicious cycle until one day you get a prognosis about your health that totally devastates you. Whatever you have been doing to yourself for so long comes back to bite you. Your health is your mind, body and soul. In the Robot level, you just exist, so you don't take care of yourself as you should. This way of thinking can really debilitate you.

YOUR INNER VOICE (YOUR INNER CRITIC)

This is what you tell yourself quietly where no one else can hear you. This little voice that talks inside your head exists in everyone. It's tied to your sense of self and it can be destructive or constructive.

There is a destructive voice that is unhelpful to you and in this level, it is loud and clear. This inner voice could have developed during childhood or from others' criticism and praise of you. This inner voice can be about your self-image, your emotions, or your abilities.

As your inner voice repeats your self-doubt, your positive inner voice gets quieter and quieter until you can't hear it anymore. Over time, you feel that your positive inner voice doesn't matter anymore so you exist in silence. What others tell you or expect from you becomes the voice you hear, and you are in an illusion of the life you think you have, but one that leaves you feeling empty at the end of the day.

Before any of these happen, you may have little signs of knowing that something is amiss, something just isn't right. Signs may come from someone telling you, or you are seeing or knowing that something isn't right. Even though you hear, see, feel or know it, a part of you doesn't really care. You turn a blind eye to it as it's easier than addressing it. You are desensitised to all around you.

The partner that you took for granted is now gone; An accident or illness changes your life as you know it; or the income you thought you could count on becomes unemployment. These are just some examples that can change your life with a bang! There were probably many signs along the way, but you may not have seen them whilst you were existing robotically. You can only avoid change for so long, and in time, if you chose to keep ignoring it, change will be forced upon you.

Once the destructive Robot level was understood, I knew I had to make decisions to change. This time, to plant a new seed – one that I believed in. Other people's opinions didn't matter anymore because I was ready to believe in me, believe in my dream. Only I could nurture and give it the right environment for it to grow. This meant sticking with my tribe, the one that had my back. The people who gave me the freedom to believe in my dream as they encouraged me to grow.

I feel I spent most of my life in the Robot level.

Looking back, I wish I had seen the signs of this level, I may have prevented an injury that changed my life, but I guess I wouldn't have understood what I do now. A few years before this happened, I had gone through a marriage breakdown and my children and I really struggled financially. There were times we lived on the edge of the poverty line. We had times when we went with no power, limited food and very little or no money. Even though my part-time job kept a roof over our heads, it didn't leave me with much after that. My memory is etched with moments within this time that kept my fear alive and powerful in my thoughts. The embarrassment of not having enough money at the end of our grocery shop because I miscalculated and left myself short was one; my children's faces as I had to take items out of the bags and decide what we needed less of for that week. I felt I had failed my children their basic needs, or that rare little luxury. It broke my heart when my children held up a packet of their favourite biscuits and then offered to put it back. With these memories, I promised myself that this was in the past and I would do better. I went from part-time work to full-time.

I found myself in a high-pressured multitasked job, and my job description kept growing as other staff members left. I was brought up to believe that I had to work really hard to have all I needed, and at the time I was a single mum with two children to support on my own. I had a dream to use my qualifications to work hard and make a good life for me and my children. Deep down I also had a dream to make my parents proud, as they had me on a predetermined path of success – married, with a big house, great children, successful job and lots of money.

Apart from having great children, I was failing miserably. The more I tried to do the right thing to please my parents, the more I tripped over.

When I found myself in this job, one where I was given so much responsibility, I thought this was part of being successful. I had to work really hard, be indispensable and please my boss. I never wanted to find myself in a financial crisis again, having to take groceries out of my bags. I just did all my boss asked me to do. This even included doing work in my own time that had nothing to do with my actual job. Whatever she asked, I did. I was given more responsibilities and I was working longer hours, and taking work home. I felt overwhelmed.

I had no one to help me with my children, so I had to leave work to pick them up from school and then go back to work again and work late to make up for the time I had missed. I felt I couldn't say no when more responsibilities were loaded onto me, and my boss continued to pressure me to take more and more on.

Later, I remarried and my family grew, and my responsibilities grew with it. I felt I couldn't speak up and ask for help with the children, my home life or work. I was taking on more than I could handle. A larger household, teenage children and stepchildren, all with different schedules. Slowly there were signs of the beginnings of burnout.

The robotic me just kept doing all the hours needed to keep everyone happy, stretching myself like an elastic band to keep work, life and household running like clockwork. I was trying to be a good mum, wife, stepmother, daughter, friend and employee but there was nothing left for me, not a drop. My work environment was slowly becoming more stressful with more responsibilities, and even though I asked for help, I kept being told no. I was so frightened of losing my job, I just kept on the merry-go-round that was moving faster and faster.

In typical Robot level behaviour, one day merged into the next and my body was telling me that something was about to give, but I just kept existing robotically as I felt there was no way out – until one day, when my body stopped me in my tracks. I took a tumble and slipped a couple of discs in my neck which impinged nerves, immobilising my neck, back, right arm and shoulder. I was in excruciating pain. Everything I feared, happened. Over the next two years, after two neck fusions and shoulder operation, I was told the nerve damage would never heal. I was told I would have to live with chronic pain, and what I feared the most happened, I lost my job. I was told I could never work full-time again and that my arm would never go back to normal. Life as I knew it changed. The robot finally broke!

Losing everything took me to the Basement, and it was in the Basement that I saw my life for what it was. It's amazing what you can see when you actually stop. Using the Basement constructively, I could see how everything around me was falling apart, but when looking through the eyes of the Robot, I couldn't see it, because I was so overwhelmed with work, responsibilities and pressure. I thought I had no alternative to what I was doing. I could then see that as my boss was pressuring me, her boss was pressuring her. So in the end, we were all robots pushing for production at high risk of problematic outcomes for everyone involved.

I had forgotten what it felt like to be happy. Thinking that I was trying to bring stability into my life by juggling and pushing myself to do it all, in reality there was no stability at all. I was conditioned to do what I thought was the right thing to do, but amongst it all I had totally neglected myself. I was failing miserably, juggling all aspects of my life, and in trying to give those around me a sense of belonging, stability, love, fun, happiness, all the good stuff, I was failing to give any of those things to myself. I understood that in saying yes to everyone else, I needed to say it also to myself. I didn't stand up for myself and say no to others when my engine was running on empty. I neglected my own needs, and the outcome was that I felt totally broken. It took me years to come to terms with my new self, which in turn opened a Pandora's box.

Over this time, I realised I had been living as a robot for most of my life, not just in my job but in every aspect of my life. I was letting fear be my compass and I was never really living. I was in empty relationships where I felt undervalued, unloved and alone, my job prospects were poor with my physical limitations, my children were growing up and didn't need me anymore...I'd totally lost my identity. The fake smile and pretending everything was okay just wasn't working anymore.

The Robot level gave me the illusion of being trapped, with no way out. It made me feel like I had no options because the options I had were so frightening to me. I just couldn't see a way out. This level immobilised me.

Once you understand the Robot, you know when you are in it. As life is never really stable, full of ups and downs, I revisited the Robot level many times and I noticed the patterns. The old patterns started to show; I would wake up every morning and I'd robotically do what I had to do but felt numb. I'd lost focus, I didn't know what I wanted, and I felt disillusioned. I lived in an impoverished mentality with low self-esteem, and accepted being treated like a no one, because I felt like a no one. I felt like a prisoner to what was expected of me, and my dreams were insignificant and therefore unattainable. I realised that my life was a merry-go-round, and life was boring – work, cook, clean, make sure kids were looked after, go to bed, do it all again. I wasn't doing anything for myself. At times I had moments thinking about the possibility of my dreams and ways I could achieve them, but then I would be reminded of the obstacles in the way of my dreams, so they just kept getting buried under a blanket of discouragement.

As part of my self-discovery I had to go backwards to go forwards. I needed to find where this robot mentality began for me and work from there. I realised my biggest teacher of the Robot was my father, who still continues to live in this level, as he has for most of his life. He worked so hard all his life. He would watch others build beautiful homes, go on holidays and spoil themselves with whatever they wanted. He would see others enjoying life, and in time it made him resentful. He lived restricted by money, so he limited himself and his dreams. My father was a gifted tailor, he made beautiful suits, but he lost hope of ever being successful and gave it up. He lost his ambition and became resigned to what he had to do. He remained a robotic factory worker doing what he didn't like, never receiving a promotion nor attaining any success at work. He did the same job for 30 years with the only recognition being a watch when he retired. There are times we have to live within our means, but being a robot is when we think we will have nothing better.

Christmas was coming and to help me find an appropriate gift for my father, I asked him what he enjoyed doing that made him happy? He said to me, 'I don't know. I don't have anything I want.' In the discussion with him he said some things that really made me feel sad for him. He continued, 'I was born to work and now that I'm old I have nothing, and I will die with nothing. I feel invisible, no one really cares whether I'm here or not. People only look for me when they need something. I'm nothing to no one.' It saddened me he would think this way whilst he had those around who love him, but he is unable to see or feel it. He feels life has gone past so fast and he didn't really get to enjoy it. When he has all his family surrounding him, instead of cherishing the moments, he is already fearful of how long he will have to wait to be with them again. Those beautiful moments are tainted with the fear and doubt in his mind, and the illusion of what he lacks overwhelms his thoughts.

Listening to my father saying to me as I grew up, 'You have to work hard if you want things in life', and now watching him in his regrets, made me realise hard work wasn't the solution. Now that he is in his 80s, he lives with remorse of all the things he never did and never had. He worked so hard all his life, and still now in his 80s he is too afraid to stop and enjoy every moment. He doesn't want to go on holidays or even have a night away. At times, he misses the beautiful moments around him because he doesn't cherish them long enough, as he focuses on when it will end and how long he will have to wait to have such a time again. He doesn't like to rest and relax to smell the roses as he feels if he stops being the robot he will die.

Over time, watching and listening to my father made me rethink my own life, as his words were imprinted in my own thoughts for most of my life. I never planned for anything because I thought what I wanted required money, and I didn't have it, so I would live in my impoverished mentality. Whenever I thought of my dreams, I would just push them aside reminding myself of the money I didn't have. I kept living in my self-defeating prophecy of telling myself I'll never have the money to do what I really want to do in my life, and life was constantly validating this 'fact'. What a vicious circle that was, as I now understand that what I think is mirrored right back to me. So, if I tell myself I have no money to do what I want to do, I will live an existence of not having enough money to do what I want to do. It's as easy as that. I appreciated that once I changed that, I could change the old ways I was brought up to fully believe in.

I'm surprised that some fears are ingrained from past generations, and some patterns are still being repeated to this day. What we learn from our parents and their parents are, their actions, their choices and their beliefs, and they can sometimes be repeated in our own generations because we don't know any different and continue the robotic beliefs and behaviours.

My belief about money and success were twisted and warped, based on the beliefs of the past, and the seemingly never-ending influence of depression. My distorted belief was that the perfect family meant I had to have money to make them happy; to be successful I had to have a lot of money and be in a high paying job. But I didn't have any of those things, I felt unsuccessful. My dream of travelling and seeing the world was impossible, as I kept accumulating so many things for my money to go on that there was never enough for me. I placed all these restrictions on my life because I thought money was the key to happiness. Wow, it still shocks me as I write this, on how wrong I really was. I thought I needed all this before I could really feel happiness and have the dreams I always wanted come true.

I waited and waited for life to provide me with what I thought I needed so I could feel whole and happy. The more I felt broken and empty, the more situations entered my life to make me feel this way. I kept feeling that if I did good, good would come back, but it just wasn't coming. I couldn't help but think overwhelming negative thoughts; nothing good ever happens to me, why me? What did I do to deserve this? I just kept feeling like life was against me. I was so stuck in this way of thinking that I couldn't see an opportunity, even if it hit me in the face. I had built a fortress between myself and my dreams with the big illusion of deficiency and hopelessness. The fortress was strong, and I slowly lost sight of my dreams.

I was a prisoner in the Robot level for most of my life, in a despondent mind-set that crushed any thought of a dream. The painful memories of my child abuse, failed relationships, disability, financial pressure, disappointments, failures, all of these were symptoms that kept me in this robotic mode. It was so debilitating that I couldn't even envisage a seed of possibility to plant in my life to attain my dream as I had nothing to give this dream a chance to grow. If I ever spoke out loud about the smallest spark of an idea, I was quickly reminded not to give myself such high expectations, to be realistic, and not to waste time or money that I didn't have. I was reminded of what I lacked by other people, and those views would crush that seed before it was even planted. I would ask for their opinion about what I should do and would listen to them because I was afraid I would make a mistake, and they knew better than me. My lack of self-belief made me think their opinions were right and mine were wrong. So, I listened to them and not to myself. My doubt in myself and my abilities stopped me in my tracks before I even took a step towards what my inner voice was telling me. Others people's doubts in me only validated my own lack of confidence. How could I believe in a dream if I didn't even allow myself to have one?

When I was younger, I used to blame my parents for what happened to me as a child. I blamed them for not being like the parents I thought other children had. The parents who should have made me feel like a child, who should have wanted to create beautiful memories with me, who should have had the patience to spend time with me and get to know me, who should have heard me and laughed with me and not at me, who should have made me feel safe and happy. Should, should, should! I was angry.

I then understood that they couldn't give me something they didn't have or know themselves. Both my parents had their own unfulfilled wants from their past. My father came from a difficult childhood. He was one of nine children in the Depression. If you woke up first, you got fed and clothed. The later you got up, the less food and clothing there was. He carries psychological scars from his past and a strained relationship with his remaining siblings. My mother comes from a past of losing her natural mother before she could walk, and this left her with a sense of abandonment from not having the bond of a mother and daughter. Once she moved to Australia from Italy as a young 17-year-old, to be with the husband she barely knew, she felt isolated and alone, and her relationship with my father wasn't love but an arrangement that gave them the opportunity to start in a new country. My mother continued to feel unloved, isolated and abandoned. So, both my parents had their own life challenges that made them the parents they became. They were so despondent and unhappy in their own lives, how could I have expected them to be there for me and see what was happening to me whilst they were in their own clouded robotic life?

For years I never looked at it from their perspective, I just felt my own emotions. It was easy to blame them because when I blamed them, it wasn't about me. I didn't have to do anything because I saw the problem in them not me. When I grasped that my own happiness was an inside job, I appreciated what my parents actually did teach me. Watching and understanding their parenting made me decide what parent I wanted to try to be. They had their challenges but also their choices, but the Robot level brought out the robotic conditioning of the past, overflowing into the choices they made for themselves. This is why we sometimes repeat behaviours from generation to generation, because we can't see that there is another way of doing things.

I realised I had choices as a parent too, and even though life threw challenges at me as a parent and then a single parent, I could still change this. I chose to give my children everything I wanted as a child and hoped for the best. Parenthood is like that, every child and every experience totally different. All you can do is your best.

I tried to give my two children a safe home and wanted them to just be kids and have fun; we not only built forts, but I got in there with them. I helped create fun memories together. I played games with them, cuddled on the couch watching movies together and we danced around on the lounge room floor. I had patience and listened to them when they said they wanted to talk. I even listened when they had nothing to say. We laughed together. We were a team; they were my light. I hid my pain from them for a long time as I didn't want them to feel worried. I felt guilt when my pain showed and they got to see how I struggled. In those times, I showed them that hard times happen and it's how we deal with those times that matter. They inspired me to always be better. I made my own choices from the example my parents gave me. I was far from perfect, and I tried to create something different out of what I started with. I got some things wrong, but I also got some things right.

I love my parents for all they have taught and shown me. Their pattern in the Robot level highlighted my own patterns that I unknowingly created for myself in parts of my life – patterns that only I could change. If you grew up with people who lived in the Robot level, you would be familiar with some of their traits. If they are destructive Robot level traits of the past, you may not even have noticed these patterns because they are familiar. However, once you acknowledge these traits, you may comprehend this Robot level and chose what you want to do.

Remember, the choice is always yours. You have to want to break this cycle to feel and truly grasp your potential.

In the Robot level, there are three options:

1. Feel the dark side of this level and over time you sink to the Basement.
2. Robotically exist here, pretend everything is okay and remain stuck or,
3. Choose to free yourself, make a change to get off the merry-go-round you have been on and do something new.

Remember the choice is always yours to make. If you are just existing in this gift of life, only you can make the changes you need to, to create something better. Are you ready to take the step to unlock your true potential? Free yourself today.

BELIEVE in that dream.

Chapter 6

HELP YOURSELF WHEN IN THE ROBOT LEVEL

CONSTRUCTIVELY BE IN ROBOT MODE

The Robot level can be a choice and a good one when appropriate. When I want to get things done, I choose to go into 'robot mode'. I give myself a plan, time limits and an expectation of what I want to achieve for myself. I did that when writing this book. I gave myself structure, and locked and isolated myself so I could be constructive. It's how I got things done. This is one way of letting this level work for me. Being constructively in this mode helps me with problem solving and planning.

IF YOU DON'T KNOW WHAT TO DO, DO NOTHING!

The Robot level can be used to your advantage for times that you are confused and don't know what to do. Instead of feeling like you have to take some form of action, do nothing until you know what to do. Otherwise, instead of being proactive, you may be impulsive and take steps that can cause the total meltdown.

Sometimes things are out of your control and there is nothing you can really do about it, so instead of worrying, accept there is nothing you can do, and take that time to be still. Instead of going around and around in your head with the 'what ifs', stopping helps you deal with situations in constructive ways instead of destructive. This means you give your time and effort to yourself, and you allow yourself to listen to your inner voice instead of blocking it out or shutting it down. The Robot can give you that time to stop and think, gather yourself for the next step.

The lower levels just require structure and limits, as they are places that can absorb you. The destructive robot mode is when you don't believe and you've lost hope. You feel tired of trying, but constructively this can be about giving yourself that time just to be still, where you don't have to try or do anything other than 'be'.

CREATE A NEW PATTERN

You are already in a pattern that's not working for you, so create a new pattern to work with. Introduce some 'me' time in your busy life. Something that is solely for you. This could be working on something that is a part of the big picture of the dream you see for yourself; introducing meditation in a part of your day; going for a walk to clear your mind and give yourself space. The Robot can be a destructive pattern, but this is a great time to make it a constructive pattern instead.

STOP AND BE AN OBSERVER

Instead of being blind to what's happening around you, be still and be an observer. Really look at your home, family, work, health, etc. In your home, is there someone who has been needing your time and support? Have you been giving your best to those who really matter? Not the tired or rushed you, the good you that you give to clients, co-workers, your boss. Instead of asking yourself, what do I get from this relationship, ask yourself what you are giving to it? If you have been in the Robot level in a destructive way, you have probably neglected those around you and have been running on empty with nothing to give to them. Remember, those who love you are your cheerleaders, they deserve the best of you. Support each other and make time to nurture what you do have. If it's family, have you had time to share with them? How can you contribute to that relationship? With work, are you working in a healthy environment? Are you happy? Do you love your job? Is the life you are living, the life you really want? Take time to observe, see if this is the way you want life to be?

WHAT DO YOU BELIEVE ABOUT YOURSELF?

The belief system you have about yourself keeps you in the Robot level. So, what are you telling yourself about who you are, what your expectations and limitations are, and where did these beliefs come from? Are they from your thoughts of your self-worth, past trauma, fear, abandonment, maybe old patterns?

Have outside sources validated your beliefs? Or has it just been an inside job?

As you observe your beliefs, what is the upside? What is a healthier way of looking at it? (From a constructive point, not a destructive one.)

This is where you can challenge your belief. Put it through a reality filter. Is it really true? This is where you can see if your belief of yourself is helpful, effective or relevant to your present life. This is where you can change your belief system – you look at each belief with clarity, dispassionately and objectively, and then change that belief. It's like a system's update on our technology. We all need a system's update from time to time, and old stuff needs to be just that, old. Time to see your belief system with fresh eyes.

Use the Robot Journal at the end of this chapter to break this belief system down.

TAKE SMALL STEPS

What makes you feel happy, fulfilled and successful? Make a list and start by making one of those things a part of your every day.

Engage in your life! Don't just contribute, be a willing participant.

If you want to travel and you can feel your limits, start small. Take a small drive on the weekend to a place you have never been. Don't let your limits confine you, look for an alternative and create memories, they last forever!

If you don't know what your dream is, just focus on the feelings you want to feel. A dream isn't a destination, it's a feeling, a place we have always wanted to be. It's how we feel that matters.

IF YOU CAN SEE IT, YOU CAN HAVE IT

Envisage change being possible, and positive for you.

See your dream, find a picture of it and put it everywhere to remind you. For example, create a vision board with what you would like in life so you can see it. When you see it, it's there in front of your eyes and not in your mind that is crowded.

Make your screen saver a sunrise or a place you're dreaming to see. Just seeing that every day will give you insight and help you connect to your soul.

HAVE NO REGRETS

People who live in the Robot level most of their lives hold regret. So have no regrets! Time is one of the biggest regrets people have. They wish they could go back in time and change something or do something they always wanted to do. Time is precious so make those special moments count.

Words not spoken are also regrets. If you want to say something, just do it. Don't regret telling someone what you really want to say – those words may never get another chance of being spoken.

Spend quality time with your children, watch them, listen to them, breathe in their precious light as they will grow up quickly and you may miss that gift you have been given. Don't let your job or your robotic ways steal that precious time with them. You will treasure those times and you will leave your children with those precious memories.

Spend time with those you love whilst they are still here. They can't wait to be a part of your life; you must be present in theirs too.

Spend time with family instead of co-workers. Work gives us money and success – it won't matter how much money you have made, how many hours you worked or all the 'stuff' you own, it won't even matter whether you were the cleaner or the CEO. It will be about the moments you created with family and the memories you hold on to and leave behind.

Don't waste time on silly arguments, worrying about something that hasn't happened or the insignificant small stuff. It won't matter in the big scheme of things.

HEAL THE PAST

Don't let the past continue to steal any more precious time. Go back in your book of life, find the bookmarks you keep going back to re-read, feel them, make peace with them, and then rip those bookmarks out! Call it the 'past', rewire the beliefs and let go of the hook that has held you there, so you can move forward freely. Your past made you who you are today, thank it. Now it's up to you to create new memories.

PASSION & WANTS

Make short and long-term goals – be passionate and ambitious as your drive will lift your energy. As you write these down, and look at them, it will be the start of making your dreams happen.

You are fortunate to have choices and opportunities that some may not have, so take the chance.

SPEAK UP

If a relationship, job or situation isn't working for you anymore, it's time to renegotiate your needs.

Stay calm when speaking up, keep eye contact and speak normally. When we get anxious or fearful of speaking up, it shows in how we speak. We then give all power to the other person simply through a fear of standing our ground. But when we stay calm and be in our truth, we speak from inside, and we can have an open and honest conversation. It is okay to speak up and say what you need, don't be afraid to. If the other person doesn't respond in the same way, that is their reaction, nothing to do with you. Speak with belief in yourself and your needs.

Being in the Robot level, you appease others and do what they want, and later you may feel resentful for doing something you didn't want to do. Honour yourself and say 'no' when you don't want to do something – have no guilt because you are speaking from your needs. Say 'yes' when you really want to say yes! Even if you feel vulnerable, breathe and do it.

TAKE CARE OF YOU

When you are in the Robot level, taking care of you can be done in a robotic way and you may be missing some aspects that are important.

Mental, physical, spiritual and emotional health are all very important, and none of them should be missed.

To keep a balance, these are some basic principles to stay on track.

- **CONNECTION:** It's so important to build relationships with those around you. These people make up what I call your tribe. They enrich your life so embrace them. In the Robot level you just exist in the relationships around you but be present for these important people, they will be there to support you. They are your cheerleaders and you need the connection to them.
- **BE EMOTIONAL!** It's okay, it's not a disease! The Robot level makes us feel numb, and we usually feel like that because we have disconnected from our emotional side. We try to avoid pain, so for some reason we think if we don't allow ourselves to feel, we won't get hurt. Weird, because if we disconnect our emotional side, we do get hurt. Emotions are important in life; they make us feel alive. Whether they're good or bad emotions we feel, feeling is important.
- **MEDITATION & ALTERNATIVE THERAPY:** Meditation promotes calm and heightened awareness. Finding that quiet time helps you connect to your inner voice, the one that has to fight to be heard in the Robot level. I use flower essences which really help me energetically with the different levels, and it's when I'm in the Robot level that I use them the most. My most commonly used essence mix is for feeling overwhelmed. It really helps me step back and see things with clarity. You can try reiki, yoga, mindfulness exercises, aromatherapy, or even kinesi-

ology. I've tried all of them and use them when needed. They are worth trying.

- **SLEEP:** It's so important to get enough sleep! If you're sleep deprived, it can really impact your mood and concentration, and you can be at risk of adverse health effects. Moods can affect how you sleep; if you have anxiety or stress, your brain may have trouble switching off, your heart beats faster, your breathing is quick and shallow. So, getting enough sleep and the right kind of sleep is important to help you out of the Robot level. Too much sleep works the same as not enough as it can make you feel even more tired.
- **EXERCISE IS IMPORTANT FOR HEALTH:** Go for a run, a swim, to the gym, a walk, any movement. This has profound benefits for your mood. If you're like me and aren't a sport freak or a runner, you can try the simplest of things. For me it's dancing. Yep, dancing. I dance every morning as my exercise. The music goes on, I dance before my shower, in the shower and out of the shower. I get at least 30 minutes of moving my body, and I enjoy it! I even do it when I am cleaning or cooking. Movement is movement in my eyes. So you can keep this one simple. If you are being robotic, it can help you clear your mind as well as your body. Get 30 minutes a day.
- **TALK TO SOMEONE:** Talking through problems is not a weakness but a strength. When we talk, we get a different perspective. We may hear something that can really help us and improve

our lives. In the Robot, we shut down, so reach out and share, talk things out. Talk, it will help you get things out of your head and shine a light on them so you can see them for what they really are.

- **TALK TO A HEALTH PROFESSIONAL:** If things get too much, and you have been in the destructive Robot for too long, get help before you get slammed into the Basement. If your relationship has come to an impasse, see this as a time of marriage counselling, seek help so it can be salvageable.

DO SOMETHING FOR SOMEONE ELSE – PAY IT FORWARD

If someone does something nice for you, pay it forward to someone else. Your action may be just the kindness they need. There are so many things you could do; holding a door open for someone, making eye contact with people and smiling. Doing something outside of yourself really helps you see life differently. It really is contagious and it's good for you!

BELIEVE IN YOUR DREAM

What is a dream? It can be a desire, a vision, a goal or something you are hoping and wishing for. Whether it's a feeling, a destination, or an experience, make sure you are putting something towards your dream. No matter how big or small, your dream is worth it. It's like lighting a fire, you must keep adding little sticks and leaves to help keep it alight. Fan it a little and keep your eye on it so it doesn't go out.

Believing in the dream will take you out of the Robot level.

ROBOT AFFIRMATION EXERCISE

Say these affirmations out loud. Emphasise the words most important to you.

I am doing the best I can.
I am free to be who I want to be.
My dreams are worth believing in.
I know where I'm going and what I want to do.
I am the master of my destiny.
I am worthy of great things.

When you finish saying these affirmations, I want you to close your eyes, and with each big breath in say or visualise what you want to bring into your life, and with each breath out say or visualise what you are letting go of. Some examples:

The Robot Affirmations

Breathe in	***Breathe out***
I bring in all possibilities	I let go of limitations
I am happy	I let go of sadness
I believe in me	I let go of doubt
I overcome all obstacles	I am free

Use this quiet Robot time as an opportunity to listen to your inner voice. See the lessons you are facing and connect to what feels right for you. Take baby steps in observing where you are right now so you can see where you want to aim with clarity. Remember, sometimes the lessons aren't clear but giving yourself some quiet time will help you see your next step, and that's all you need. One step at a time, and then know what to do next.

YOUR ROBOT LEVEL JOURNAL

Use this space to write about your belief system that keeps you in the Robot level. What destructive beliefs bring you here and how you can constructively change these?

What are you telling yourself about who you are, and what your expectations and limitations are? And where did these beliefs come from? (Self-worth, past trauma, fear, abandonment, maybe old patterns.) Outside sources or inside job?

Chapter 7

THE STRUGGLE

This level is when you are at war with yourself. You want to break free from the Robot but you have past limitations and a negative inner voice that continues to stop you from moving forward. This is where the true inner battle begins. It will make a warrior out of you!

The Struggle begins when you choose not to be a Robot anymore. It's as simple as that. You have finally decided you want better for yourself and you want those Little Luxuries that you know you deserve. You're tired of the merry-go-round and want to get off and take a different path. Being there for everyone else is great, but you are wanting to be there for you too.

When you are on the merry-go-round, you keep getting the same lessons but in different situations, and you find you are always back in the same place you started from. In the Struggle, you decide to break this vicious cycle. You need to take a new path, one you may have never travelled. You may feel apprehensive when you get off this repetitive ride because you may not know which way to go. But taking this next step is important for you to bring change into your life, as you know you can't be a robot anymore, you deserve better.

View the Struggle as being a crossroad in your life. The Struggle is standing at a crossroad, where moving positively towards what you want intersects with looking back at the path that you are so afraid of letting go. Overwhelming feelings of guilt and fear of change; what will it mean? These feelings may quietly call you back to the Robot. Change feels scary, difficult and too hard, but you know you want better, and this is the level before great things start to happen. You may worry about actually doing something for yourself and may feel guilty about placing yourself first. This is the calm before the storm, with the storm heralding the emergence of *the you* that you so much want to be.

It's easy to give up in the Struggle, because fear raises its big head in this level and it still feels too hard to reach what you want to accomplish. What you will learn is that you are not just existing anymore, you're wanting so much more for yourself and need to look at ways to change and take those small steps toward what you really want. This is a place where you will question yourself, your abilities and your worth, and find the strength within you that you never knew you had. You will question yourself in many ways in this place and wonder if you will gain anything by pushing through this hard level, but rest assured, even though the Struggle appears to be difficult, it's the most crucial part to your personal growth. This is where hope, trust and self-love is born.

The Struggle can be seen as the crossroad between your limitations and your possibilities. It's a place where you need to decide where you want to go by trusting your own instincts and your gut feeling to guide you. 'Trust' is your lesson in this level. You may find that in life you have placed trust in others who have let you down, but you haven't placed trust in the most important person of all, you.

Making decisions and choices can often create great anxiety. You may think about the risks you may need to take, you may question your decision and intention, and worry if it's the right decision that you're making. Your inner voice, in the Struggle, really wants you to just go for it. Sometimes you have to be ambitious to get to where you want to be, have the will, battle the doubt and push through the fear of change to see what you're made of. There is a warrior inside of you who can handle this.

In the Struggle level, your fears are heightened as you aren't sure what you are supposed to do next. Are you going the right way? You don't have to know where to go in this level, it's all about learning how to trust your own instinct and follow your intuition to where it may lead you. You may not see where this path goes but building that trust in your own decisions and guidance will always lead you to where you need to be. You will have decisions to make along the way, so trusting your path to guide you in the right direction is learnt in this level.

The Struggle wasn't my favourite level when I realised I was in it, but over time I knew what I had to do. Little by little I had to strip away all the layers I had from my past, my pain and my expectations of what I thought I would be. Layer by layer, making myself raw, vulnerable and going deep to finding my true self. The old me was dying as the new me was emerging. This happened many times, and each time I became aware of my feelings and listened to my intuition. I understood I was in the Struggle because decisions needed to be made and change was important for me. I realised that life had brought me to an impasse where I had choices to make. I always knew it was for my greater good. As you change the Struggle will appear, giving you the opportunity to release what you no longer need, trust yourself and follow the next path placed before you.

The Basement left you helpless, the Robot made you exist, but the Struggle will finally bring your fears to the surface. You are given the opportunity to overcome these fears by recognising them and identifying where they came from, and through your own intuition, trust and faith you are able to dissolve them.

Perhaps they are things you have been told in the past – people telling you that you are not good enough or that you will amount to nothing. Or actions people took towards you that made you feel afraid of moving forward. Some are stuck in the Robot level because they are afraid of change so it's safer to comply and be robotic and not change. Even though the Robot level brings them nothing new, it also keeps the fear under control by being a 'safe' environment, where you may not like it but it doesn't change. That is not living, that is allowing your spirit to die. Whatever the fear or restraint, you need to know what it is and understand why it's there, and have the courage to step into the Struggle – feeling the fear but wanting to be free to change.

The Struggle can be an internal belief system that could have been created in your childhood, where you were being told who you were before you even knew who you were. Maybe it was your parents, sibling, friends or a person who said something that shaped a picture in your mind of who you were supposed to be. Those words can scar you so much that every time you want to bring forward change, you hear those words so loud that they feel like hooks pulling you back so you can't move forward, and if you do, you feel pain. It's about identifying what the hook is so you can go back, feel it, heal it and move forward.

This hook may be from a past event, which in your own life story book becomes a bookmark. One that you go back to over and over again, and it's easy to find. It becomes your reason, your excuse, what holds you back from getting off that merry-go-round. Every time you want to do something new, you start off well, but as you move forward that hook reminds you of where you came from – it limits your movement as the discomfort becomes too much. You feel it, you talk about it, and internally you stop and go back to that place again and again. The hooks from your past continue to control your movement forward until you can identify them, see them clearly and heal them. Until you do that you cannot move forward.

This level opens your eyes to your negative thinking and self-criticism, and you become aware of the things you say to yourself and how they make you feel. This pattern and energy empowers and controls your fear. Within the Struggle, you will actually hear your negative inner voice question where it came from, challenge its validity and want it gone.

I have had past clients who have said they thought they didn't have any fears but they just couldn't seem to move forward. They thought their obstacles were external influences or barriers stopping them from being where they wanted to be. However, when I saw the way they negatively spoke to and about themselves, the poor choices they made and the self-punishing they did, it was quite obvious their obstacle was an inside job. It's easier to look outside ourselves because we don't have to be in control of that, and if we look within, we may not like what we see. However, it's in the looking within that we truly see the magnificence we possess.

Negative self-talk and name calling is destructive! Stop criticising yourself! This affects not only your mind but your whole body and the energy around you. You are like a magnet – everything you feel, you radiate and then the universe responds to that energy you are putting out – so you attract everything that validates what you feel about yourself.

For example, if you say, 'I hate my job', your body responds with symptoms of stress and anxiety to anything to do with your job. That energy is released from you outwards, and those around you can feel your negative energy. Then the universal energy responds; you attract more situations to give you more reason to hate your job when you are there. It is a vicious circle in all aspects of your life.

If this is something that you are going through in your job situation, change the saying to, 'I love my job'. Your body doesn't feel the stress when you say that, and your energy is more positive even though you are in a job you don't like. As your energy changes, a new job may be offered to you or a new opportunity may arise because you have changed the energy of your circumstance.

I was talking about this very thing in one of my group sessions, and one of the girls was in a job she didn't like at all. She knew the workplace she wanted to work in, but she couldn't see how she could ever make that happen. She was continuously attracting more and more things to dislike about her job. Her office door was always closed to shut the world out and she wanted to be left alone. Her mental and physical health was suffering. So, I suggested she change her morning affirmation to 'I love my job'. Initially she laughed out loud! She found that funny and thought it would be impossible to do as there wasn't a single aspect of her job she liked, but she decided to humour me and did it. Over time, as she said 'I love my job', she decided to rearrange her office, so she had a view of the garden outside the window. She then progressed to keeping her office door open, and began to feel lighter at work. Because her door was open, one of the doctors who worked at her place of employment saw her and invited her to work in his new office, which was at the workplace she was hoping to work at! She totally turned her life around with a new positive thought and moving away from a job she didn't love to a job she had hoped for. The Struggle lets you look at the positive, but you have to put the work in to make it happen. Trust is the key.

One of the times I found myself in the Struggle was a few years ago. I had been in a Robot episode, which was my way of dealing with the memories of my childhood abuse. It was a big taboo subject and one that wasn't spoken about. This particular part of my past had me living in the Basement and Robot levels for most of my life. I struggled to see past the memories of this part of my life, which kept me in these two levels. I felt that the universe was encouraging me to shine the light on this part of my life, rather than be lost in its darkness. I couldn't let it destroy me anymore and leave me frozen in these levels. This was my big breakthrough out of the Robot and dealing with it in the Struggle.

I kept seeing my abuser's daughter come up as someone I may like to befriend on Facebook. Even though I had fond memories of her from my childhood, the memories of her father were horrible, but as he had passed away, I wasn't overwhelmed with fear, but I was overwhelmed with the memories and how destructive I felt about myself. My guidance was about 'coming clean' with her. A part of me thought, maybe she had gone through what I did. I had written to her father many years before to tell him what I thought of him, it was a part of my excruciatingly long healing process. It was an outpouring of my anger. I didn't put my name on the letter as I knew he would know who I was. My name was not necessary. I wondered if he had spoken about it before he died, so, I reached out to her. I told her what her father had done to me, not in too much detail, as just opening up about it was hard enough for me at this time. I prepared myself for a rejection because of all the things he had said to me and that no one would believe me. When you are ready to move forward in the Struggle, you begin the change that is best for you. So I didn't let his past words affect me since at that point I didn't really care if anyone believed me or not. It was about healing myself because my anger, resentment, betrayal and all my self-loathing emotions were destroying me physically, mentally and emotionally. I had to do this for myself.

She surprisingly replied with shock, as she was the one to receive the letter many years before and had never shared it with her father. She thought it was a hurtful joke. When she realised it was from me, I could tell from her reaction how sorry she was. She wished she had confronted him about it but unfortunately it was too late.

It gave me an opportunity to open up to my mother about it after many years. It was so cathartic to open up but at the same time it left me empty. I took a turn for the worse at this time. There was a part of me that thought, he didn't suffer. Yes, I did want him to suffer then. I wanted him to feel the fear that I may tell others of his abuse. I wanted him to know I had grown strong and that his secret would come out. But I fell into the Basement very quickly, and after a while I just lived as a robot again as there was nothing I felt I could do.

In time, I decided I just couldn't be robotic about it anymore. Even if he did get my letter and read it, I wouldn't have done anything beyond that. I just wanted to empower myself in knowing that he knew. It was just my anger at him for what he had done to me. It wouldn't have changed what he did to me, or how it made me feel. Nothing can take me back to that little girl, wipe it all away and let her be the little girl she should have been free to be. But, I could work with what I had left from this big life experience, I could come clean for me and only me. My beautiful friend Heidi, who worked at our radio station, was recording podcasts and writing about real life stories. She asked me to write my story. She thought it was going to be about my psychic journey, my angel work and the readings I do, so she was shocked to read that it was about my childhood. The #MeToo movement was emerging at this time, so it seemed like the right time to bring on the change. I was scared, but I did it. My story was out, after 45 years there were no more secrets.

In choosing to do this, I identified the Struggle level. I wanted to let go of the anger, the resentment, the betrayal I felt inside that was eating away at me. What I wanted was freedom from it and little by little it happened. Our unresolved pain in the Robot eventually takes its toll on us and it affects our health too. My past was making me sick, and when my gallbladder was taken out I found out it was at the stage before cancer cells began. My surgeon said cancer in the gallbladder is one of the most painful and untreatable. I researched it and found out that anger, frustration and bottled up resentment is held in there. I then understood that holding all this in was going to make me sick somewhere else. So that was the beginning of the process to heal.

Going through the Struggle was a struggle! I wanted to by-pass the emotions of this level, yet my pain kept taking me back to many things that had happened to me at that time. I had forgiven my parents years before this, as the resentment of them not keeping me safe from him was destroying our relationship. It wasn't just them, there were others who knew but did nothing about it. I had to go back to that chapter in my life and begin the healing process. It was hard as I felt like I was reliving it all over again, but I was seeing and learning a lot about how it was affecting how I was living now. My past was keeping me stuck in a submissive life. I had to go back and forgive myself and others. My mother would say how I must have suffered when I was little and she wishes she could do something, but I reassured her that she couldn't. I didn't want her to feel guilty about something she couldn't change now. I told her I was not angry with her anymore. I now know that without what I had been through, I wouldn't have become the person I am now. I started to see my strength, and how much I had endured throughout my life – the relationships I was in and the circumstances I attracted. When you feel submissive to life, life gives you more situations to be submissive to. The more aware I was becoming about myself, the more I knew I had to be strong for myself. I went back to my childhood, found myself and I promised that little girl that I would always put her first. I would make her happy, I would make her feel safe and I would love her as much as she should have been loved.

I always had that hook from my childhood that stopped me from moving forward. It kept me stuck in a place where I was scared, controlled, obedient, a good girl doing what I was told. She always felt she had to do what everyone told her to do. Whilst in the Struggle, I began to understand this hook and feel it wanting to hold me back, I also saw the little girl that I had made a promise to. She became my reason to heal and move forward. I took her hand and she moves forward with me every day.

So, you see, you can't just look at your dreams, you also have to look at your nightmares.

The Struggle is not just about your dreams and finding a purpose, it's also about facing your demons, your nightmares, they are the obstacle that will continue to be in your way. Whatever your demons or your nightmares have been – fear, the past, pain – they need to be healed or you will feel the hook constantly pulling you back to the Basement or the Robot. The more you avoid dealing with your demons and nightmares, the bigger and more powerful they become. You aren't here to suffer; you are here to live your best life. The universe continues to bring you lessons to learn so that you don't keep pushing these nightmares away, or burying them deep inside you, otherwise they will come back fighting you harder each time. You have to go back to go forward, so this level pleads with you to do this for yourself.

I had a vision that helped me to understand what it was like to let go of my past abuse before I did it. When it came to my child abuse, I was in a prison all my life, stuck in this vicious cycle of Basement and Robot, and I was ready to set myself free from this place that was safe but trapped. In this vision, I felt the fear and excitement fighting inside of me as I stood on the step of the prison gates wanting to be free. I had only ever known what it was like to be in the prison. Looking outward made me feel scared with all the 'what ifs' of the Robot. What if I won't survive out there? What if I put myself out and someone hurts me? Will I be safe? There were many fears to hold me back but the 'what if I don't do it' was scarier. What if I stay stuck and never feel freedom? So in amongst the fear, I took the first step to freedom and the gates closed. I had forgiven my past, I had forgiven myself and I was ready to move forward and let the freedom flow through me. As my energy within changed, the energy outside of me changed and the universe responded. All I had in my life that kept me submissive began to fall away. I was not a prisoner anymore, and I didn't want to be treated as one. I promised myself that I would never be made to feel submissive to anything I didn't want ever again. When you get on the path of the Struggle and you invest in healing and change, the universe aligns with you. The Struggle becomes one big stepping stone in changing your life.

In this level, you understand energy. Not only do you feel the energy within you that you are putting out, but you can feel the energy surrounding you too. Maybe negative people or gossip sessions just don't feel good in your energy space anymore. The energy in your workspace, friendship groups or relationship, clash with your own energy. This doesn't mean you stay away from them; it just means you are becoming more aware of your surroundings. The Struggle awakens your senses. As you can feel, hear and see the negativity happening within you and around you, you begin to align with what feels good for you, and change begins.

This is the level where you start to follow what feels right instead of doing what's right. You begin to make choices that are right for you. Honouring your intuition will be so important because you are following your own radar. It always speaks to you and tells you what to do but you usually question it or ask for someone else's opinion because you undervalue your own. You may even fear what feels right but listen to yourself! You know what to do!

The Struggle is where you find commitment – commitment to you. You commit to others, in a relationship, to your children or to a job...but why not to you? Here is where you make the decision to commit to your cause.

Instead of waiting for something to happen to you, you decide to make it happen for you. Do you want to keep waiting for your life to begin? Do you want to keep waiting for that perfect job, that perfect relationship, that slim body, someone to love you and appreciate you? Seriously! You have all of that right now inside of you! Don't hide your beautiful light from others. Release your beautiful essence of who you are. Waiting wastes time. Living life is now.

This level is the make or break time! It's where you commit to yourself or you just fall back into being a robot and exist for everyone and everything else.

Beginning the Struggle is where you no longer choose to be a robot, you want better for yourself, you want Life's Little Luxuries and aspire to be connected to Awesome Source. It's the Struggle to stay positive whilst the Basement calls you, because this is the level where the real work gets done. When things feel too hard, it could just be the time before great things start to happen. We usually give up in the Struggle level because it feels hard. We question ourselves. We wonder if it's even worth pushing through each difficult moment, but it is. It's one of the most *important* parts to it all. The median strip, the middle ground, the crossroad.

You have ambition, but you don't know where to start. We all doubt our potential at times and have fears that keep us stuck.

The Struggle was my most challenging phase. The constant drop to the Basement was frequent and exhausting, but at that point I knew I deserved more and I was tired of the repeated lessons. I knew I wasn't here just to exist. I could have died a few times but I was still here. I was meant to be here. I was worth being here! This is where the desire to better my life was born. The drops to the Basement became less and less destructive, and more and more constructive, and I would go down to recuperate and prepare myself for the next battle.

Fighting the ego, the voice in your head that tells you that you can't do it, is a challenge. Please don't fear the word ego, as I believe there is a healthy and unhealthy ego. Using that ego in a negative way is thinking that you are superior to others or you rate yourself higher, but a healthy ego is about having self-esteem and self-importance in a loving way – knowing who you are, and your value in this big world. We have been taught in the past that being selfish was wrong, yet we failed to see the importance of 'self' for growth. As you learn to face all the challenges you have had in your life and how you have grown and strengthened your relationship with yourself and others, you will see how much you have enriched your life with meaning.

As you become more in touch with who you are, you will see what your purpose really is. Your purpose is not a negative ego-based trip. It's not about power, control or manipulation, it's about boundaries, listening and trusting. Your purpose isn't what others want for you, or think you would be good at. It's where you make a commitment to yourself, where you have faith and trust in who you are and at peace with your own existence. Your purpose is *your* inner voice that knows what it wants. It's okay if you feel lost and don't know what your purpose is right now, as sometimes we have to get totally lost before we are found.

It's important that you don't waste your time being confused by external shiny things as they dull in time – you are much more in control of your inner shine. You are of value. Don't force things to happen, let them happen. It's not meant to be perfect but it's meant to feel right for you.

When we come to a stage in of our life where we are questioning our purpose or our destiny, we are in the Struggle. I found myself stuck there when I was searching for my life purpose, like it was a destination. I went from group to group; I did so many workshops and classes in search of this big 'purpose', which I was sure was going to come to me like an epiphany! The search only made me more and more confused, my passion heightened one moment and then hard to find the next. I became passionate about everything I did, but in time it began to fizzle out because passion was a feeling not a purpose, and it would leave me deflated. I realised that finding my life purpose was more than status, career, being rich or successful. My purpose was about just trusting myself, believing in myself and the path I was on. When I applied my sense of purpose to what I wanted, things changed.

TRUST in who you are.

So, What Are You Afraid Of?

There is always a reason why you were stuck in the Robot level and chose to make a decision to bring about change. Maybe you also had an epiphany, an aha moment, and you can see that you want change and want to do things differently.

Now that I am aware of the Struggle level, I know I have had numerous signs pointing the way out of the Robot level, but my fears were too powerful to release me to make changes. When change is inevitable, there will come a time when you have no choice but to change. You give in to it because you know it's best for you.

When one of my best friends was diagnosed with brain cancer, it was life changing not just for her and her family but for her friends and everyone who knew her. She was younger than me and she was my sounding board. The friend who didn't really mince words, she said it as it was, hard and straight to the point. The friend you need who kicks you in the pants when they see you aren't loving yourself. We spent a lot of time together, and she told me so many home truths about what I was doing to myself that I knew she really wanted me to do something about it. I was reminded of how I kept putting everyone before me. I opened up to her about my childhood abuse at this time, and she helped me understand my fears and how they continued to manifest themselves in my life. She shared with me what she wanted me to do in this life, and I promised her I would. I was so scared of making changes. I focused too much on what others thought of me, how it would affect my family and I worried about making a mistake. Of course, fear still had its grip on me. Facing the Basement's dark side woke me up. I realised I was about to let go of a beautiful life and let my fears win. The switch went on. I thought, I don't care what others think of me, I have to live in my life every moment of every day, and if I'm not happy, I'm the one who is losing out. My friend's words were loud in my heart. She told me to stop being scared, and my inner voice agreed with her. No one was going to hurt me anymore because I wouldn't let them. She was an amazing teacher and an exceptional friend to me, and I will always cherish her honest and loving advice. She is still my sounding board.

So, are you ready to face your demons? Because this is where your story really begins. You decide what you want to be and where you want to go, you.

(Make notes in the Struggle Journal space at back of this chapter.)

- Do you know what you want to change?
- Do you know what stops you from taking steps towards it?
- If it's fear, what are you afraid of? (Making a mistake? What others think? Failing?)
- Are you afraid of losing someone or something?
- Are you afraid of change, and if so, why?

- If self-love is hard for you, what is your block? What have you heard, seen or felt in your past that has created this boundary for you?

- If money has been a hurdle for you, what is your block? What have you heard, seen or felt in your past that has created this boundary for you?

- Do you self-doubt and/or sabotage your abilities? (If yes, how?)

- What's your hook that keeps holding you back from taking that next brave step?

The Power Of Positive Thinking

The old proverb, 'I become what I think about all day long' is what you are attracting into your life. Be aware of this and you'll start to be really careful about what you think about.

Positive thinking is important when breaking through the Struggle. Negative thinking is what you have been trained in, and now you have to think the opposite! You are turning your thinking on its head.

We are always hearing about creating a positive life but what we try to do is force ourselves to do something we aren't feeling. We push ourselves into thinking that we need to think and feel like someone else. But we are all so very different so we can't all find positivity the same way and in the same things.

Removing that expectation is very liberating, as positivity comes in many forms and is unique to the individual. For some, just waking up brings positivity as they may have been unwell or suffered an accident that left them with a fear of dying. For others, when things go right, it brings on positive thinking. However, if your plans go wrong, it's so easy for negativity to come flowing in. It's about accepting what just 'is' and knowing that if it's not right for you right now, it can be right for you at a later stage, so never give up.

In the Struggle, you will start to hear your negative chatter, because you are aware of it now. Learning how to think positive is a step at a time process, especially if you were brought up in a negative environment. Positive thinking initially can feel like pretending, because you are saying something that isn't aligning with your situation. But I'm sure on bad days when you were asked how you were, your response was, 'I'm good thanks', when in fact you weren't. So sometimes to 'Fake it 'til you make it' can work. I chose to do this. I didn't know what being positive was going to feel like, so I had to start with simply deciding to be positive.

You decide that you are going to be positive! Whatever it takes. It grows on you. You are going to see your possibilities, your strength, your accomplishments – yourself – for who you really are.

Whenever you notice yourself thinking or saying a negative thing about yourself or your life, replace it with a positive.

For example, a common one I hear a lot is, 'I'm stupid'. No, you're not stupid! Replace that negative ego phrase with, 'I am kind', 'I am unique', 'I am loved'.

Make an easily accessible list of three positive things that remind you of three uplifting things about you. Don't limit yourself to three but start off with those and add as you grow. Every time a negative judgement comes into your inner voice, let your powerful inner voice remind it who you really are. You're not fighting with the negative chatter, you're showing it who you are, and in time, the negative chatter will lose belief in what it thinks and quieten down, because it knows the powerful inner voice is right.

Positive thinking re-programmes your negative thinking, and when you acknowledge your fears, they become tamed. This way you re-programme your mind not to jump to a negative conclusion every time.

Don't run away from something you think you can't master. If you think positive thinking is unattainable, then you will never have it. Positive thinking is easy, it's a phrase you tell yourself every day to empower yourself. In time, it will be a normal thing you tell yourself. You can retrain your thoughts.

Don't ever think there's something wrong with you, because there isn't. Focus on all the things that are right about you, there are many of those.

You need to believe you deserve it; visualise it in your mind and heart, and trust for it to be so.

Affirmations are a great start in this phase, because this is where you want change for yourself. This is where you say, 'I am willing to heal my past and bring joy into my life'.

It's small things that create big changes – as simple as, 'I love myself and I deserve a beautiful life'.

You have the power to bring positivity into your life.

Through the Struggle, you make a decision to want to be free, to want to take the steps to bring forward the experiences you want and to trust the process.

Chapter 8

HELP YOURSELF IN THE STRUGGLE LEVEL

YOU VALIDATE WHO YOU ARE, NO ONE ELSE

When you need other people to validate who you are, you have seriously lost yourself. YOU validate who you are, no one else.

MIRROR WORK

Sometimes you need to be told you are loved, or that you are beautiful, or that you are accepted just as you are. The most powerful person to tell you this is you. Looking into your eyes in the mirror helps you to connect with your soul.

Many people don't really look at themselves in the mirror. There are things they don't like to see or acknowledge about themselves. They find fault, so they robotically look in the mirror to get something done but not to really look.

I really struggled with this, as I would only look at myself in the mirror to put make-up on or do my hair, but I never really looked at myself. I would always notice all my flaws, lines, spots, imperfections but never my good points.

I didn't realise how much negative internal chatter happened in front of the mirror until I was in the Struggle level and I could hear it.

I wondered what could happen if I changed it to positive talk instead.

I started with, 'I love you Rose, just the way you are.'

It felt weird, unusual and that I was telling myself a big fat lie!

But I kept doing it, even though I didn't like it for a moment. One day, I started saying it and I burst out crying. I couldn't stop crying because I realised how hard I had been on myself. I was hurt when others said hurtful things to me, but I never realised how hurtful I had been to myself. I actually looked at myself and said sorry to myself. I apologised for all the cruel things I had said to myself over the years and that it was going to stop right there, at that moment. And it did.

Mirror work helped me a lot during my healing from my child abuse.

I would say, 'I am here for you, protecting you, listening to you, loving you and I will always have your back.' It really helped me with the healing process. When I look in the mirror these days, I compliment myself on the things I love about myself, my qualities, and sometimes I just laugh because I have a great sense of humour. I even dance in front of the mirror. Thank goodness there are no cameras as it really is funny, and my inner spirit glows with happiness that I can be myself.

The mirror doesn't lie, and it reflects how you feel about yourself. You will start to see more than a superficial reflection. You will start to see an inner glow or an inner emptiness. Whatever you fill yourself with will show itself.

Fears and doubts are also reflected back at you when you look in the mirror, and you can use mirror work to help you with your past.

If your fears or doubts go back to childhood, try this:

See a little you around the age of five. Think of what you were doing at that time. Think of how you felt about life. If you were happy, remember that and know she/he is still inside of you. Tell her/him all you needed and wanted to hear about yourself. Tell her/him what you have done with her/his life. And if you feel that you missed telling them something, take a note of that. This will be part of your healing.

If you were going through negative and painful experiences at this age, I want you to really see this little child looking back at you, feel her/his pain and then reassure her/him that you are here now. Apologise for not being there to save her/him before, as you were still learning to be brave but now things are changing. You are here to protect her/him and that you love her/him. And that no one will ever, ever hurt them again.

When I saw my little self for the first time, she was dark, lost and looked despondently back at me. She had been left behind, wondering what she had done wrong and why no one was there to protect, save or love her. I cried for her as I would never let anything happen to any child, but I left her there in my memories in the dark. I kept the mirror work going and it took time for me to talk her out and to remind her that I never left her. When I told her I am here now, I won't ever let anyone ever hurt her again, she was brave and began to lose the darkness. Through my Struggle, she went in and out of the dark as I grew to trust and love myself so that she felt that she could trust and love me too. I listened to her whilst she told me her pain and in my heart I held her and told her it was okay. I wanted her to feel safe and to open herself up to life and not lock herself away anymore. As I grew, so did she. Over time, through mirror work, she was freed. The mirror helps you work with you, your past and who you want to be.

If your fears or doubts go back to an accident, or a time in your life where fear and doubt were created, you can do mirror work this way:

See yourself at the time that you felt the fear and it stopped you in your tracks, reflecting back at you. Look at yourself and how you were dealing with what happened to you at that time. See how fear and doubt took over and your spirit hid in the dark and you became a robot and just existed.

Tell yourself that you are here now. Apologise for not being strong enough then to know what to do, but you know better, and you can do better now. Close your eyes and visualise holding close that hurt self, like a lost friend you haven't seen for such a long time, and give yourself love. Put your arms around yourself. Let yourself trust in you again. It will take time. The old you needs to believe in the new you, the one that isn't going to give up until the old you is healed.

Be gentle with yourself through this transition, it may take days, weeks or months but it will happen.

For today, look in the mirror and say to yourself, I love you just the way you are.

AFFIRMATIONS

Affirmations are the words you say to yourself. When I ask people if they know what an affirmation is, they say I don't do them. When I hear them speak negatively, I say, 'Umm that's an affirmation'. You are telling yourself that you are not good enough, so you are attracting situations in your life that validate you are not good enough. The faces they pull after that is quite funny – usually shock. What you say to yourself is an affirmation and that's a good reason to say something that will work for you and not against you. An affirmation opens the door to possibilities. It can either help you eliminate something from your life or help you create something new. So, they are quite powerful. Use them wisely. There is a list of them in the next section, the Struggle Affirmation Exercises.

POSITIVE THINKING & POSITIVE SELF-TALK

Positive thinking is important, so whenever you notice yourself thinking or saying a negative thing about yourself or your life, replace it with a positive, or even three positives! Change the energy from what you think and say.

Stop name calling and criticising yourself! This doesn't only affect your mind but your whole body and the energy around you. You are like a magnet so everything you feel you radiate and then the universe responds, so you attract it.

ENERGETICALLY PROTECTING & SHIELDING YOURSELF

Energetically protecting and shielding yourself is important in the Struggle level. We take out insurances with the expectation that our home, belongings, car and health are safe. We take vitamins for our health to protect us from bugs and we put a seat belt on in the car to protect us from an accident, but do we ever think about our energy space?

Negative energy affects your thinking, how you see life and what you do with it, so protecting and shielding yourself is very important.

If you work or interact with people who are feeling lost and confused, your energy is vulnerable to absorbing their energy. This is also important for people who interact with those who are unwell, unstable and negative, such as nurses, doctors, teachers and counsellors, or for those who work in a hospital, police force, courts, funeral parlour and many more work places. Think of the industry you are in. Do you connect with others or are you in a negative environment?

Protecting your energy is a part of self-care. Only you are in control of protecting yourself from other people's energy. When you place protection around you, you can interact with others without it affecting you.

There are many ways of doing this, but I like to keep it simple.

- **Set healthy boundaries**
  If you are feeling vulnerable and have people around who drain your energy, listen to your intuition and keep your distance until you are feeling better. This could be if you are tired, unwell or feel-

ing flat because your boundaries are vulnerable at this time. Self-care is about taking care of yourself and stepping back. Saying 'no' when you don't want to do something is part of this.

- **Pull the plug**
  If you are around negative surroundings, when you leave just say, 'I lovingly release and disconnect to what doesn't serve me'. If you can visualise, see a plug between you and the person or situation you have walked away from and pull that plug. Release and disconnect.
- **Ground yourself**
  Go outside, take your shoes off and get your feet in the grass, on the earth, on the sand. Ground yourself. When you are grounded, your protection shields are stronger.
- **Archangel Michael**
  If you are an angel person like me, Archangel Michael is my security angel. He keeps me safe and protected no matter where I go. He can't help you if you don't ask. So, if you need him, call on him saying, 'Archangel Michael, please protect me now'.
- **Crystals**
  I love crystals, and for protection I use smoky quartz. Others that I have also used that are great are obsidian and black tourmaline. Wear them, put them near you, even in your pocket. Keep them in your energy field.
- **Work with light – protection shields**
  This is my most common way of shielding myself. When we work with light, it comes in different

forms and colours, and all of them are significant to you. You are not just facilitating protection, you are also letting the universe know what you're actually needing by using colour. Listed below are shields of colour that you can use for yourself and for others.

Light	Purpose
White/Gold	Gold is the ultimate protective shield. White can be used against crime or physical attack. This shield also calls upon additional angels to around you. I place this around myself, my family, my car or/and home.
Pink	This shield only brings in love. If there is conflict between those we love, place pink around it. Pink is the colour of unconditional love so use it when you are finding self-love.
Green	Use the green shield if you are sick or injured. This can be even used on others. Friends, family, pets. It is the light of healing.
Purple	This shield provides protection and shields against anything negative - negative thinking, negative people or environments.
Mirrored ball	When you're feeling vulnerable and you're about to go into a harsh energetic environment (such as crowds of strangers or an intense meeting), see or feel yourself stepping inside a mirrored ball. Like a disco ball. All negative energy bounces away from the ball.
Lead	Even though lead is heavy, see the colour and know its lightweight yet so strong. This is an ultimate shield against negativity whenever a battle is anticipated or you're feeling extra vulnerable or open. See or feel yourself completely surrounded by lightweight lead metal which nothing can get through.
Triple Shield	Pick three or more of the colours and layer them on top of yourself for ultimate protection. There is no right or wrong way to do this. Follow your heart in what you feel that you need.

THE STRUGGLE AFFIRMATION EXERCISE

Say these affirmations out loud.
Emphasise the words most important to you.

Positive changes are happening for me – I am unstoppable!
I am co-creating with the universe to achieve my goals.
I let go of old habits that are limiting my potential.
I pay attention to my inner voice and what it's telling me.
I'm on the right path taking me where I need to go, I trust the path.

When you finish saying these affirmations, I want you to close your eyes. With each big breath in, say or visualise what you want to bring into your life, and with each breath out say or visualise what you are letting go of. Some examples:

The Struggle Affirmations

Breathe in	***Breathe out***
I bring in new and positive experiences	I release old habits that limit me
Positive changes are happening for me	I let go of doubt
I am on the path to achieving my goals	I release fear
I deserve this and I am ready!	I let go of negative thinking

Use this reflective Struggle time as an opportunity to see where your past robotic habits started from. Go back to your past to heal so you can move forward freely. See the lessons you keep facing and encourage yourself forwards. Quietening the negative voice and gently nurturing it with your positive voice will strengthen your spirit. Give yourself time, and be gentle with yourself whilst you are learning how to trust in yourself and your path.

TRUST in who you are.

YOUR STRUGGLE LEVEL JOURNAL

Write here about your fears, doubts, past words or actions that stop you (or stopped you in the past) from moving forward. Do you have any negative inner words you tell yourself? Use this space to reflect on this level.

Chapter 9

LIFE'S LITTLE LUXURIES

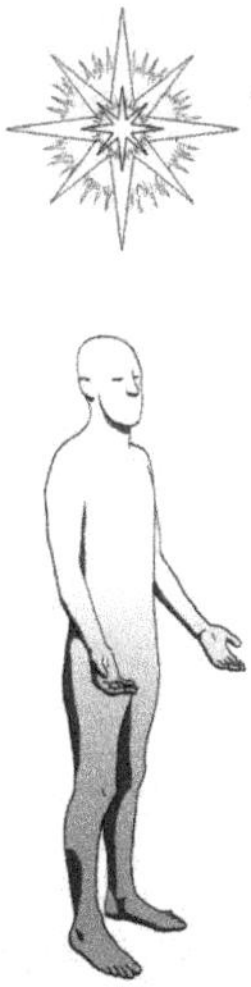

It's amazing what can happen when we chose to be gracious. When we are grateful for all the little things in our lives that we take for granted, we open up the door of opportunity for so much more.

Life's Little Luxuries is the level where we appreciate the little things. Those things that usually get unnoticed – that sunrise and sunset that happens every day – but when you do stop to watch them happening, you can see their beauty and feel their presence.

We often take so many things for granted and focus on all the things that are going wrong that we may miss the beautiful things that happen around us every day.

We live in a very abundant world, yet we focus on all the limitations and things we don't have. My eyes were opened when I visited a Third World country where I realised being rich isn't about money. We have it all wrong! I was the poor one when I saw how happy and close to family these beautiful people were. I watched the children close their eyes to the wind blowing on their faces and laugh as they played with their friends in the street. No electronics, just fun playing with a plastic ball. I gave a young boy some money and he ran to give it to his mother who would use it to help feed her family. He didn't show any selfishness but was selfless. It was definitely a different world to the one I lived in.

I had to be careful with the water I drank and where I walked. There were times I felt afraid of my surroundings, yet everyone around me looked so happy. Over time I realised I had taken so many simple things for granted that when I returned home I began to value everything.

I valued that fresh clean water, straight from my tap in my kitchen. If I was hungry, I had food in my fridge. When I went to bed at night, I was safe in my home and in my comfortable bed. I had air conditioning if it was hot or cold.

I could walk around in the streets in my own familiar surroundings and feel at home.

I began to cherish my family and friends even more, as I realised that in many ways technology was replacing our physical connection. I always had my phone stuck in my hand but there were times I began to forget where I had put it. This was because I started living in the present moment and being a part of this world.

I had been struggling in the Struggle, but now that my eyes were open to seeing all the little luxuries that surrounded me, I began to feel gratitude for so much more.

Life's Little Luxuries is about being grateful for what you have, and how it opens your eyes to the world around you, giving you more reason to feel grateful.

I always worried about money, and I would check my bank account many times a day, as though something would miraculously happen. I did it because I was afraid of not having enough. When you trust that you are blessed with life's little luxuries, you have confidence that your needs will always be met, and that worry will get you nowhere. I learned that when I feared money, I put up a barrier to it, and money didn't flow into my life. If anything, I was preventing it coming to me. I learned to trust in myself in the Struggle. I let down the barrier of fear and my eyes were open to Life's Little Luxuries.

This is the level where you see what you do have and don't worry over what you don't – in all aspects of your life. You start to see all the hidden blessings.

If you are not in a relationship and are waiting for the love of your life to come along, instead of worrying that this love hasn't come yet, you will see the love that already surrounds you. When I was in this level, and I realised I was comfortable within myself to be by myself, I felt blessed to be a part of those around me – my great girlfriends with whom I would catch up over dinner or coffee and quality time with my family. I was already in loving relationships, and instead of focusing on the love I didn't have, I opened up to the love I already had. In time, the right love came into my life, which was just what I deserved and had always wanted.

I used to think that life's little luxuries was going on holidays in the winter time. We used to call them winter breaks, and we would go away for a couple of days, take the kids down to the bush and stay somewhere that had a fireplace – that to me was one of life's little luxuries! But it was more than just the holiday, it was about quality time with my children – cooking a slow-food meal, fetching firewood and playing board games at night. It was family connection with no technology, no distractions and one-on-one time with my children where we could enjoy each other's company. For us this was truly a luxury.

Life's little luxuries are moments of joy that can easily be missed in the hustle and bustle of daily life. When you take time to notice these blessings you will see how many there really are. Some of these things you may take for granted, for example, electricity, hot water, flushing toilets!

There are people who spend most of their time feeling they don't have the life they really want, but when you think you don't have the life you want or deserve, counting your blessings helps you to appreciate that your life is full of life's little luxuries.

This is the level of feeling thankful for what is in our lives. It's that simple. Brooding or complaining about not having what you want doesn't get you very far. Remember, what you put out you get back. Use this time to be grateful for all you have and all you are. That gratitude will be returned to you a thousandfold.

When we are grateful for love, we attract more love.
When we are grateful for abundance, we attract more abundance.
When we are grateful for our loved ones, our time with them is more enjoyable.
When we are grateful for our health, we are happier.
For a miserable wet day, we get rainbows and our plants are watered. Don't let what you think is gloom in life become gloom, see its blessing.
For every dark night there is a new day.

We evolve in this level; we have the opportunity to change old patterns and create new ones. The more things you look to be grateful for, the more you will find.

Being grateful changes you. No matter how dark life feels sometimes, when we feel grateful, we can't let a negative feeling in. Gratitude is powerful, be grateful to evolve.

Gratitude changes you. These are some of the things you may notice.

WITHIN YOURSELF:

1. It makes you more optimistic and you can discern many more blessings. When we are optimistic, it

makes us happier. We begin to focus on the good in our lives instead of thinking about the bad.

2. It can centre you and help you feel more spiritually awake and open. When we are grateful for our lives, we are connected to our spiritual side/religion/God/universe. We just feel a connection to something bigger than us.
3. You will feel happier and more content. This has been shown to improve our health, and I've read studies that say it gives us a longer life. I must say that with some people I have known in my life, it's been those who have been grateful who have passed away happier with no regrets. So, I see this more as, if you hold many regrets in your life, you aren't really living, you are existing. Let go of regrets and you will be living your best life.
4. More relaxed within ourselves. Anxiety and stress feel tight inside our being and makes us tense and blocked. Gratitude and breath let that tightness go and bring a sense of peace within.
5. Gratitude helps mental health. Many years ago I was diagnosed with chronic depression. As I learned more and more about gratitude, the more it helped with my mental health. Over time, as I practised gratitude, it rewired my thoughts and I slowly overcame the 'chronic' part and now have much better control over my thoughts. I have seen clients who practise gratitude cope and manage their mental health so much better. Recent studies by Portland State University and Clemson State University

proved how beneficial gratitude has been to those who are suffering mental health issues.

6. Better self-confidence and self-esteem. An example of this; You will feel open to accept kindness instead of wondering if there is an ulterior motive for it. You will see that you are worthy of help and kindness from others. It also makes you look bright, and people's compliments make you feel better about yourself. Once I began using gratitude every day, I noticed many people telling me how happy and good I look. It sparked a feeling of joy inside me, which was so different from the past feeling of negativity. It was so refreshing to receive a compliment and be accepting of it.
7. Sleep and feel better. Due to my pain and injury, my sleep was broken and difficult most nights. Feeling grateful has helped with not just sleeping but my quality of sleep. I go to sleep faster and wake up refreshed and happy.

WITHIN YOUR RELATIONSHIPS:

Deeper and more respectful relationships. Let's face it, people like happier people. Happy is contagious. If you are moody, angry and complain a lot, others are not drawn to you. Gratitude makes us nicer people to be around. It allows trust to deepen and it connects us on a deeper level.

1. Acceptance of others. Practising gratitude makes you kinder and friendlier toward others. As you feel better about yourself it radiates outwards like the ripples in a pond. You accept others for who they

are and understand them better. When we are grateful for those around us, we appreciate them so much more.

2. Less envy and more empathy. Instead of looking outwards and seeing what others have and focusing on them, you are grateful for what you have. You start to look at those around you in a more selfless way and with compassion instead of envy. Gratitude also helps you feel less materialistic and helps you see others beyond their material possessions. We are more than things.
3. Creating happier memories. Whilst there is no perfection, gratitude allows us to see the good parts in memory making. It's so easy to recollect our bad memories, but gratitude helps us to recollect our good ones.
4. Feeling good when you are with friends/loved ones. When we are grateful for those precious people in our lives, instead of dreading the time we *have to* spend with them, we feel good with the times we are together. This helps us to create magical memories to recall later on. When we feel good to be around others, they respond with enjoying it too – it's win-win.
5. You will see your blessings in your relationships. When you are grateful, instead of seeing what is wrong in your relationships, it allows you to see the blessings these people bring to your life.
6. How can you be judgemental of people you are grateful for? It's impossible.

WITHIN YOUR WORK:

1. Enjoy your job more. Seeing all the positives in your job/career helps you to enjoy your job.
2. You will connect better with others at work as they will be positively attracted to your energy. You can work more as a team member as you will be able to see the positives in others' abilities. We live in a world where we are called into an office to be reprimanded rather than being praised. Gratitude helps you to influence change in letting others feel good about themselves because you feel good about yourself. Bring out the best in others as well as yourself – it will make you more passionate about your job.
3. More confidence in your decision making. You will trust your ability to make decisions, feel confident when they need to be made and to stand by them.
4. Manage your job and time better. Time management and job satisfaction go hand in hand when you love what you are doing.
5. Achieve goals you set for yourself. If you are striving for a promotion or better job, being grateful for where you are will help you achieve your future career goals.
6. More efficient in your work. Gratitude helps you to be so much more productive in a job when you see its value.

Gratitude is such a big part of not only seeing life's little luxuries, but helping you attract more of them into your life. Some wait for the big things in order to feel thankful but it's for all the little things in life that we should be thankful. Big things are great! But it's the little things that are so easily missed. As I stopped and thought of what I wanted to be grateful for, I found it hard to start. I began this process by being grateful for three things every day. I found that in time I became repetitive and I really was limiting myself with what was around me that I totally took for granted. I sat down one day to write a list and I was surprised of all the things that I really was thankful for. I would add things to the list on days I noticed the luxury of having it. Like when the power is out, your internet is down, or the water is turned off for the day. You really notice the things you take for granted on those days. I even noticed people when they went on holidays and weren't in my life for a period of time. I also noticed the luxuries when I went on a diet and had to avoid certain foods, or when I made a choice of giving up something I liked for Lent.

I would love to share my list with you because it may help inspire you to write your little list down in the Life's Little Luxuries Journal section at the back of this chapter.

I wrote this list and keep it in my journal for the days I am visiting the Basement. As I read them it helps me fill my cup of gratitude and helps me climb out of the Basement with ease. I could have kept writing these, and your list will vary and include so much more that I have missed. Here we go.

My Grateful List

1. My parents – for creating me. Without them, there would be no me.
2. My children who have taught me about real love; what it feels like, its depth and the lengths I would go to see them happy. The realisation that there is no end of love for them and the true meaning of unconditional. And their partners, who have blessed me with more to love, and my grandson who lights up my world every time I see his beautiful face, hear his cheeky voice and hold him in my arms.
3. My partner in life who loves me, has my back and supports me for who I am, fully. He understands all I am going through and just knows what I need. He listens without me speaking. He won me over with 'I would drive hours just to spend a moment with you.' And meant it.
4. My tribe who are family and friends, and no matter what, they are there for me and love me.
5. Coffee! Yes, it comes right under my people. The smell, the warmth in my hands as I hold it and drink it. Ahhhh, it's heaven for me.
6. My eyes that show me the magnificence of a beautiful rainbow and breathtaking sunset. That I see the love that surrounds me.
7. My ears that hear the giggle of a baby, the sound of beautiful music and the words 'I love you' from those I cherish that fill my heart with happiness.

8. My hands that can touch, hold, feel, type and scratch an itchy spot!
9. My sense of smell that can savour the aroma of a home cooked meal and my white sage incense in the air. The smell of fresh rain and the ocean when I sit by it.
10. My taste buds for the sweetness of fresh fruit, the salt on my lips after being in the ocean, tasting a new food and eating my favourite food. Did I say coffee? Coffee excites my taste buds!
11. I have a voice to express myself. I can talk, laugh and sing! Well I keep the singing to myself as my tone isn't for everyone's frequency. Ha ha!
12. My heart that has been beating since it was in my mother's womb that keeps me alive. My heart feels my emotions, whether I love or hurt. It is in my life to show me that I am alive.
13. My lungs that breathe life in every day and that have helped me blow up the balloons for my children's birthdays.
14. My legs that take me where I need to go. I walk, skip and jump with them. When I go for a swim, they help me move through water. How I cross them when I sit and play with my grandson. Shoes for protecting my feet.
15. The sun that rises and sets is the most glorious to watch. The sunshine on my face that warms my soul.
16. Thank goodness for music! I love dancing to it every morning and it totally lifts my spirits and sets me up for a wonderful day. Lyrics can emotionally move

me to laugh or cry, and can empower me when I need a lift.

17. I love my bed! It's my spot where I can just rest and rejuvenate for another day.
18. Thank you for a toilet that flushes and the toilet paper that goes with it.
19. I'm grateful for my mistakes, my heartbreaks and my tears. They all showed me where I went wrong and how I could become better as a person. They taught me that I needed to trust myself more and showed me my value.
20. Internet for connecting me to people I would otherwise never have been connected to. Aren't we lucky to have technology!
21. Having love in my life and lots of laughter that makes my tummy hurt!
22. I love my work. I love working with my angels, with the universe, and all it includes. I love how I can just be myself and connect with them and all I feel is love. I am so grateful for being aware and open.
23. I am grateful for my life and everything in it.

This is just some of my list! I have so many things on there as it's a work in progress. I can find things to be grateful for every moment of every day.

Look around, see all of life's little luxuries. You are surrounded by them every moment of every day. They're in the air you breathe, in all you touch and all you are.

In this level, you change, grow and take a step upward from the person you used to be. Your awareness opens and you are accepting of life and its beauty.

THE NEGATIVE EGO

The negative ego may pop its head up in this level, so if you see and feel all of Life's Little Luxuries surrounding you, say thank you. Don't allow it to go to your head or make you feel like you are better than someone else in a big-headed way. Being boastful or arrogant isn't working from light.

Chapter 10

HELP YOURSELF IN LIFE'S LITTLE LUXURIES

PRACTISE GRATITUDE

Being grateful is easy, but being grateful as a choice is a trait that takes time and practice. Gratitude changes you gradually, sometimes without you noticing, but others notice. Initially, you start with small things like water, your bed, family, food, etc. but over time you start seeing how blessed you truly are, and you live a thankful life. Gratitude is a learning progress where in time you can find things to be grateful for instantly without really having to think about it. With time and practice your feelings will intensify and be long lasting. Gratitude will help you bounce back from the Basement as you grow through your times of anxiety and stress.

START A GRATITUDE JOURNAL

Every day write three things you are grateful for in your own journal. This doesn't have to be an elaborate journal; it can just be a simple notebook. Keep it beside your bed, on your office desk, or close to where you might sit for a few minutes every day to write and reflect. You can write in it at the beginning or the end of your day. Initially, I recommend you write in it once a day. I found it best at the end of the day as I reflected on my day and it was easy to think of three things that I was grateful for every day.

A GRATITUDE JAR

I have a gratitude jar that sits by my bed. I write all the special memories or things that happen to me that make me feel grateful. In Basement time, if the negative words are floating around, I get my jar and tip all my notes out and read them one by one. After a few, I feel my smile, and my heart connecting emotionally to those memories. Gratitude just helps you remember the real things. This can be a jar, some people I know have a box. Whichever feels right for you. But this is the place where your gratitude notes remind you of the amazing things you have in your life and of the magnificent person you are.

CREATE A GRATITUDE RITUAL

Before you eat your meal, be grateful for it. It helps you notice and appreciate what you have. When you wake up, feel grateful for waking up and having another day of life. See the blessings of being in a safe place while you slept. Some see this as a blessing, and some take it for granted. When you step into a hot shower on a cold day, feel the heat and how it warms your body and how it makes you feel. Be grateful. It is the simple things – shelter, warmth, food – we take for granted and don't appreciate how precious they really are. Noticing these things will help you open your eyes to what you have to be grateful for in your life every day.

HAVE A GRATITUDE STONE

This can be a rock or crystal that you carry with you. You can put it in your pocket at the beginning of the day and take it out at the end of the day. Whenever you touch it, give thanks for something in that moment. As you put it in your pocket, have a morning thanks, and when you take it out at the end of the day be thankful for something from your day. This just gives you a physical reminder to be thankful. I have always used rose quartz as my gratitude stone and it is the stone of love.

WRITE A THANK YOU NOTE

This could be to your partner, your loved ones, a work colleague, anyone that you feel may need this appreciation. Just a little note to say thank you and share with them the appreciation you have for them. Make it a habit. As you use affirmations to become connected with you in the Struggle, this becomes a way of being connected positively with those around you. This will build a stronger bond with those you love and appreciate. It eliminates regret, because regret is something we may never be able to fix. Writing a thank you note can make someone's day which will fill you with warmth and love.

SPEND TIME WITH YOUR LOVED ONES

These are your people. These are the ones who miss you when you are doing your own thing. These are the people who have your back, will put their hand out to lift you up and would hold you when your world has fallen apart. This is your tribe. These are the people who don't want things from you, they want time. Moments of memories to build, laughter to share and hugs to have. These are the people who are a part of you, your DNA, your energy, your family.

If you are having problems with one of them, instead of avoiding them, feel gratitude for having them in your life. Once we feel that they are here to teach us something or you teach them, it makes it easier to step forward. They may be the way they are because of their own make-up, their own experiences, and they may need someone like you just to help them feel significant. When you are with them, take the time to listen to them. Really listen, not think of what you are going to say next because you aren't really listening when you are doing that. For whatever reason they are a part of your life – hearing them, being in their space, may be just what they need. This act of gratitude shows people you care. In this technology-based world, we have lost the art of face-to-face listening and bonding. Make a point of doing it.

PRACTISE MINDFULNESS & MEDITATION

Sit down for a few moments daily, close your eyes and think of things you are grateful for. Picture these things in your mind. As you sit there and picture these things, and the feeling of gratefulness fills your soul, take it in. This powerful practice helps you to manifest more of what you are wanting. The more you feel and see all the things you are grateful for, the more they are attracted to you.

PLEASE & THANK YOU

This was something I was brought up with but it is becoming a simple act that is disappearing. When you ask for something, say 'please', and when receiving say 'thank you', it means a lot to people. Don't succumb to the negativity in the world, become the change and be consistent. Appreciation and kindness go a long way and give you and others something to be grateful for.

VOLUNTEER

Giving back to others in your local community or in your work helps you be more grateful for all you have. Choosing to volunteer to help others helps your own wellbeing. This can be helping the homeless, the elderly, animals or children – wherever there is a need or wherever you feel your purpose is. It could be collecting blankets before the winter comes and donating them to support groups to help others, food collection, helping in a kitchen or reading to people in a home. Remember that helping others helps you.

There Is A Destructive Part Of Life's Little Luxuries

Every level has a constructive and destructive aspect to it and even Life's Little Luxuries has its own duality.

THE INNER CRITIC

If you haven't worked through the bottom three levels constructively, you can choose to jump to Life's Little Luxuries without working through your fears and nightmares. If you don't work though them, it may wake up the 'the inner critic' and bring forward the negative side of gratitude. This is where you may feel guilty about asking for what you want, and for having what you do have, the things you are grateful for. These are old patterns that just need more work in the Struggle level. Remember how you felt unworthy, not good enough and negative about yourself for years? It will take time to rewire your past, to change, take your next step forward. You deserve Life's Little Luxuries!

IF YOU CAN'T FIND THINGS TO BE GRATEFUL FOR, TRY JUST KINDNESS

If you are in Life's Little Luxuries, and you are having trouble finding things to be grateful for, this level can make you feel like you must be failing in some way. You're not! Keep your gratitude going but address the fears that are still coming up for you in the Struggle. Guilt and/or feelings of not being worthy enough take time to heal, so instead of feeling like you have to be grateful for everything, try just the act of kindness. You will find gratitude along the way.

DON'T BE A GRATITUDE PUSHER

Another destructive attribute to this level is wanting to get everyone else to do it too. Being a gratitude pusher is not what Life's Little Luxuries is about. You may see all the things to be grateful for, but it doesn't mean that everyone else can see them too. If those around you are going through difficult times, they may not see life as you do because they are in their own level doing what they have to do to survive. It's important not to be forceful with others about gratitude. This is something everyone will find within themselves when they are ready. Think back to when you were in the Basement, if you knew anyone that was in Life's Little Luxuries level, and they began to tell you how wonderful it is and that you need to do it too, how you would have felt? You probably would have totally avoided them. Your own journey is just that, your own journey. When someone is in a dark place, and you tell him how lucky they are, they won't agree with you. No matter how you tell them. Pushing others to do what you are doing can be destructive as they will feel more of the Basement emotions because they don't understand what you are feeling or doing. The most beautiful thing you can do at this point is just be you. Live the way you are – if they want to know more they will ask. They have to be ready just as you were.

DON'T COMPARE YOURSELF TO ANYONE ELSE

Sometimes, when you are feeling grateful, doing affirmations and trying to create the life you are wanting, you begin to compare yourself to someone else. They are not you, and you are not them. Don't start this journey with your best friend and think it will be the same because it won't. You have already been on a different journey; you are different people and have a different purpose in life. You can support each other but you won't be the same, you are unique.

THE NEGATIVE EGO

The negative ego may pop its head up in this level, so if you see and feel all of Life's Little Luxuries surrounding you, say thank you. Don't allow it to go to your head or make you feel like you are better than someone else in a big-headed way. Being boastful or arrogant isn't working from light.

LIFE'S LITTLE LUXURIES AFFIRMATION EXERCISE

Say these affirmations out loud.
Emphasise the words most important to you.

I believe the best is yet to come

My life is full of so many things to be grateful for.

I am grateful for everything in my life.

I am surrounded by love and positive people.

The right people always come into my life when needed.

Everything I deserve will fall into my lap.

When you finish saying these affirmations, I want you to close your eyes and with each big breath in say or visualise what you want to bring into your life, and with each breath out say or visualise what you are letting go of. Some examples:

Life's Little Luxuries Affirmations

Breathe in	***Breathe out***
I invite gratitude into my heart	I let go of fear
I am thankful for all I have	I let go of not having
I appreciate all that life brings to me	I am not afraid
I see all of life's little luxuries that surround me everyday	I let go of limitations

Cherish your Life's Little Luxuries and let the attitude of gratitude change your old way of thinking so that your eyes are open to all that surrounds you and flows through you.

Life's Little Luxuries is a time of transformation.

YOUR LIFE'S LITTLE LUXURIES JOURNAL

Write or draw here what you feel thankful for. Was there a time when you were without something and when you got it again you realised how grateful you were in having it again? This is your space to share with yourself your own gratitude list.

Chapter 11

AWESOME SOURCE

When I ask, I am heard.
When the time is right, it is delivered.
Every cell in my body is connected to universal energy.
We are one.

When I initially saw this title, when this book was given to me, I thought Awesome Source was about winning Lotto, a big promotion at work, earning a lot more money or any financial gain.

If you were unattached, it meant that perfect person would come along and change your life. It would be meeting the love of your life.

In health, you are given a clean bill of health.

Basically, whatever you are wanting and hoping for in life is Awesome Source.

I saw this place as one where all those dreams and wishes you hold in your heart break out and come into existence.

I would love to say to you it's all these things, including the Lotto win, but who am I kidding? When I received this book, I felt my life was a cesspit, and Awesome Source would be all the things I thought I was missing. It was all the things I had ever wanted and dreamt about – well what I 'thought' I'd always wanted and dreamt about.

But over this past year, I realised I couldn't finish writing this book until I really understood what Awesome Source was about. It was the chapter I stopped at. I thought it would never be written as I didn't understand this level completely.

What I did know was that Awesome Source was that awesome feeling of being connected to the Source, be it God, angels, guides, universe – whatever you feel your source is. I also understood that it was the knowledge and belief that the universe's energy in its totality is available to me and working with me. I also realised that it was more than things, stuff and money. It was about connection, peace and a sense of belonging. I'd never really felt like I belonged anywhere, but this level brought me that feeling that I could only have ever dreamt about.

What did belonging mean to me? It was that feeling of being accepted, heard, nurtured, understood, and with all my faults I was loved and cherished anyway.

I thought that Awesome Source, was all about material things and luxuries but it was so much more than that, as I discovered.

I'd heard about Zen from some masters and mindfulness from other people, and there *is* such a place. A place where you are comfortable in your own skin. Where you are sure of who you are and what your purpose is. You listen to others, yet you have the final say inside because you know what's right for you.

I had thought so much about this level, of what I thought it was going to feel like before I actually experienced it, but in the end all my preconceived ideas were nothing like what the level presented as.

We spend so much time hiding, existing or struggling that by the time we get to gratitude, we are just exhausted because life is hard. Life is supposed to push us when we are wanting to achieve whatever is our vision of Awesome Source. But we can't reach this place without being dragged through mud, falling into dark pits of hell and working so hard on ourselves that we finally fall to our knees before we are strong enough to actually stand. It's taken me almost all of my life to stand, truly stand. Sometimes we have to go through the darkness to see the light and to then believe that it was there all along.

Awesome Source exceeded my expectations. It affected many aspects of my life and I wasn't even remotely prepared for what it all was about. Awesome Source meant that everything I was thinking, and everything I believed about myself, I was attracting. Situations were coming into my life to close off my past. In the Struggle I was ready to heal, I was ready to let go of my past and the old ways, how I had lived my life was changing. I had spent so much of my life as a doormat where others seemed to wipe their feet, where everybody just expected me to be there for them all the time. It was as though I was on their path not my own. I so desperately wanted to be on my own path, and I accepted that I was there for them, and that was okay, but now it was my turn. I didn't want to hold the regrets of the past like my parents have. I wanted to live the best life I could with no regrets. That meant I had to follow my heart, I had to do what was right for me and it was time to make my own decisions and not let others make my decisions for me.

It all started with my own home, the place where I feel safe, my sanctuary. I almost lost this home as I was struggling financially on my own and I didn't know where I was going to get the money to be able to keep it. The housing market was very depressed and if I did sell, I would have lost whatever money I had invested. Because of my disability from my injury, I couldn't work full-time to be able to maintain such a mortgage by myself. I was trying to learn and adjust on how to live by myself for the first time in my life. I'd always had someone with me and all of a sudden I was alone. I was always afraid of being alone and what that might mean, but I learnt it was all about finding the real me.

During this time I had to really dig deep and work out how I was going to save myself and my home. I feared what would happen to me, the thought of living out of my car and where I would go. I was desperate and feeling that I couldn't do it by myself, and thought maybe I'd made a mistake by listening to my own intuition. As my self-discovery progressed and I learned my value, my self-worth, my marriage ended. I had hoped that instead of walking away, he would fight for me, work it out with me but the opposite was happening. The relationship was becoming toxic, and my inner voice and everything around me was pushing him further and further away. I had to trust that maybe it was the way it was meant to be, but during the time that I was about to lose everything, I wondered if I had done the right thing. In listening to what my guidance was telling me, maybe I'd made a mistake, maybe I should have stayed in a difficult relationship just for the sake of having a home and not being alone. I was pushed to the edge, but instead of doubting myself like I did many times previously, I chose to believe that my guidance was right and I kept walking down my new path.

You see, the Struggle taught me I was worth believing in, my gut feeling was worth trusting, and I was stepping into a place I'd never been before. Leaving the prison I had been in all of my life meant I had to trust myself, I had to believe in the guidance I was receiving. So when I took that step I believed. I believed in my dream, and I trusted myself, and when I started to use Life's Little Luxuries and express my gratitude and feel grateful for everything I had every day, my life started to change. Every day I woke up with a smile on my face and I would say, 'I'm so lucky I get another day.'

I appreciated everything I had, from the air I breathed to the water I drank and the food I ate. I was grateful that my heart was beating because it had the will to face another day. I had a courage I never thought I would have, and after dark, when I could hear the sounds of the night, instead of being afraid I knew I was safe.

Being grateful for my life and everything that was in it allowed me to start evolving and changing. I stopped feeling fear like I used to, I stopped doubting myself and I stopped questioning the path I was on, I knew my life was in my hands and I was in control of it, no one else. I didn't want anybody else to be in charge of *my* life ever again. I wanted to control my life, make my own decisions and follow the direction I was going.

Opportunities that came to me on my path enabled me to avoid losing my home, but it took courage to step out and ask for help. But when I asked, it was given. Then it was my health, and I asked the universe to please help me with my health, and it was given. When it came to relationships, I never really thought I deserved a good relationship. My concept of a relationship based on what I learned as a young girl wasn't positive as I'd watched my parents struggling on their own in a poor relationship, so I had no idea of what a good relationship looked like. I had relationship fantasy from watching TV, and based my thoughts on something that wasn't real. Instead of basing my beliefs on other people's relationships, I knew I had to start from the beginning again, so I began to build a relationship with myself.

When I looked at all the love I had given to my previous partners, my children, my family and my friends, I decided it was time to add my own name to that list and love myself.

I started to realise how much I'd neglected myself for most of my life, but deep down I knew I didn't want to be alone, I had a lot of love to share with another, but I wasn't going to end up in another relationship like I had before. I didn't want to be on someone else's path, only my own. I wanted to be with a partner, someone who had similar dreams to aspire to, and who was strong in their own right and made me feel safe. Someone who would celebrate my triumphs and wanted to hold my hand and my heart during the down times. Deep down I wanted to believe there was such a person. I believed I deserved a partner who would cherish who I was and who I could love right back in the same way. I always thought love was supposed to be difficult and have obstacles because my relationships always did – from not being accepted, to difficulties with blended families, and always feeling like I was unwanted, not appreciated, because that's really how I felt about myself. This time I did love myself, I did accept myself, I did trust myself and I knew I could bring some value to another relationship.

I never thought I could actually manifest something like that because I had pretty much given up on love completely. Love to me was pain. My last relationship almost cost me my life. I felt like it ripped everything out of me and I thought I would never be able to put myself back together again. It almost destroyed me. I could hear that little girl inside me hoping she would be worth fighting for, and instead of someone fighting for me, I fought for her, for me. I guess we are always looking for that knight in shining armour; someone no matter what, who will come back and say I love you so much, I want to work on this and I will do anything to make this work. I thought that was just in a fairy tale. I remember hearing that phrase, 'I would travel hours just to spend a moment with you'. I thought that was definitely a fairy tale. But fairy tales do come true, but only when you know that you deserve that fairy tale and you are worthy of it. It's at that point that someone who sees love as you do enters your life. Someone who's willing to meet you halfway, someone who's willing to travel hours just to see you for a moment. Someone who sees your value and cherishes you. I never would have believed I could say, 'You can really create this Awesome Source.' It made me realise how the universe not only heard me but responded to me.

Awesome Source is an amazing level where there is no limit to what we can create, because if it's meant to be for you, it will be. You can only receive what you think you're worthy of as Awesome Source can only give you what you think you deserve.

Affirmations, manifesting and gratitude don't work until you know and believe that it is possible. When you ask for what you want, you believe you have been heard, have faith that it is coming, and you will receive what you asked for. In all aspects of my life I have learnt that Awesome Source is more than the things we seem to ask for; money, love, career. Awesome Source is about connecting and being in tune with the universe's energy that surrounds us, that responds to us. When your energy and the universal energy come together, we are in synch and we become a part of the universe and it becomes a part of us. We are one. I remember being told that the universe was abundant and anything we ever wanted was just a thought away, we just had to tap into it. That was about 15 years ago. I never really got it, I never really understood how to tap into that universal bounty, and I had tried everything. I was being grateful, I was manifesting, I had vision boards. I did every Law of Attraction course, I read books, I listened to podcasts, I just couldn't get it. I didn't know that it was so simple so I was making it overly complicated. I was missing in the equation. You are the key that unlocks this abundance. If you don't think you are worthy of it, how can it come to you?

When I asked, I heard the answer loud and clear, it really was within me just as the answer is within you. When you become at peace with who you are, you love who you are, you listen to your own intuition, your own gut feeling, you trust the process, and you are grateful for everything that you have – you begin to truly align to what the universe has for you. You align to that big abundant source that is there for you. It's true, whatever you put out comes back tenfold so be really mindful of everything you do.

Do good and it will come back, do bad and know that the universe has a karmic response. In time, all the good you do comes back to you. I always hear people say, 'But I'm a good person, I've only done good things, but good things just don't come to me'. Until you believe that you are worthy of it, it won't come to you. I would love to say that everything will come to you when you ask, but it won't if you don't believe it, if you don't trust. Until you are fully aligned with who you are and believe in who you are, the universe is constantly blocked in giving you what you dearly want.

This isn't about stuff, things, this is about how you want to feel. How do you want to live your life? I promised myself I would have no regrets, and I have made the choice not to have any regrets.

I realised I was an empath but I was being a destructive empath. This meant that I allowed myself to be a doormat, a martyr, I put others' needs before mine, I allowed others to drain whatever energy I had because I had no boundaries. I allowed people to come and use me for whatever they needed and then they would disappear and I wouldn't hear from them until they needed me again. I realised it was my purpose to be an empath in this world, but I had to find a constructive way of helping. If you are here to help others it doesn't mean you give everything of yourself and leave yourself with nothing. Being a constructive empath means you have boundaries, you have limits, because you love yourself enough to never leave your tank empty. You balance your energies, so what you give out you bring back in – it's important for your health, it's important for your mind, it's important for your soul. Being an empath means being there to empathise with people, to help them. You know how they feel, you know their pain, you relate to them, you honour them, you hug them, you listen and you help wherever you need to help, but you must give that back to yourself to be a strong empath. Your purpose may be to help others, but your duty is to make sure you are healthy and able to do that job.

Awesome Source is when you understand the path you are here to follow, the purpose you have. Purpose doesn't mean destination; purpose is understanding who you are and using what you're good at. Then you utilise what you're good at to be a part of this world. You know it's something deep within you.

When I found my purpose I thought it was going to be about reading people's cards to help them through their problems, but I realised I am here to help others in many ways. I let them know that I get them, I understand. I came to appreciate in Awesome Source that everything I had gone through from a young age – the abuse, the pain that I have gone through in relationships, friendships, family – made me who I am today, because whoever comes to see me I have a glimpse into what they're feeling, and they seem to know that I know.

When people are in pain and are opening up, they instinctively know when someone really gets them. I know my purpose is to help others because I understand. You can go to many therapists who are straight out of university with a degree but if they've had no life experience they are treating you from a book. They are great facilitators of understanding the human mind, but they can only help you as much as you are willing to help yourself. They are treating you from a middle ground statistical perspective, but you are not a statistic, you are an individual and you are unique. No two people are the same and what you have gone through and the struggles you have faced are unique. Everybody feels and reacts differently. You can seek help to guide you, but no matter how many years of therapy you do, if you are not willing to change, heal and grow, you will be in therapy all your life because you are not willing to do anything with that information to change your life.

Awesome Source is where, over time, you have collected lots of information and guidance and then you piece it all together until it feels right for you – what makes you tick, who you are. You have to believe in who you are to have the life you really want because without that self-worth and belief you will keep chasing your tail until *you decide* I am ready to change.

Every time you come to Awesome Source in the beginning it's just simple things like the birth of a baby, a wedding, a wonderful occurrence that make you happy. The happiness comes and goes and sometimes you don't think anything else good will happen to you but the ultimate Awesome Source is when you just align with the universe, when you and the universe connect, when what you really have been waiting for, comes. For example, if you are wanting a change in career and you put your thoughts out into the universal atmosphere, the right people just seem to be on your path and they offer you what you want, taking you where you want to be. Sometimes you may feel lost and think you are in the wrong place at the wrong time, but instead it turns out to be the place where you meet the person you were meant to meet. When our thoughts entwine with the right circumstances, miracles do occur.

Whether it's angels, Ascended Masters, God, or gods, whatever feels right for you is right for you. Follow the guidance you're getting. The universe doesn't care what religion you are, what colour you are, if you're big, small, rich, poor, short or tall, the universe is magnificent. It only feels our energy. It responds to our fears, our doubts, our emotions, and to our light. It responds to whatever we emanate.

This is the dreams-come-true level; the level we feel we will never reach or that we don't deserve. But that is far from true – this place exists for you.

This could be the opportunity that changes your life for the better. It could come when you least expect it. It can be anything from, 'I'm pregnant! I'm going to have a Baby!'

The second you lay your eyes on your baby, that's Awesome Source. That most incredible feeling. This can even be when it's your own grandchild and you see your own children all over again. It's that heart exploding joy.

We are all capable of Awesome Source. We all deserve Awesome Source! Don't ever think that this is not for you because it is for you, for me, for your family, friends, neighbours, for everybody! Awesome Source is available for EVERYONE! Never, ever deny yourself. Never, ever feel you don't deserve it because you, my dear friend, deserve all levels of awareness because you are whole and you deserve all that this life has to offer you. No matter how good or bad, it will make you, not break you because you were not brought into this world to be broken. You were brought here to bring forward your magnificence. Never forget that. Never forget who you are because you are unique.

Awesome Source, for me, is when the universal source works through me. I couldn't write this book until I had truly lived this level.

Awesome Source is when you can truly be you. You come clean about life. You don't hide behind fear and ego anymore. You want to be you, no mask, no fear...just authentically you.

When we are in this level, we can see and feel how it all makes sense; the why we need the down time; the times of having to just go with the flow and make no changes but just breathe; the desire for change and what you were prepared to risk or fight for, and the blessings on how to appreciate the small and simple things in life.

This chapter took me the longest to get to, and I was afraid I would never truly be in it. I had seen glimpses of

Awesome Source in my life but I didn't realise that learning about all the stages would allow this level to impact me as much as it has. I always wondered how I would feel being in this level, and what if I never really arrived there. I asked myself if I would ever experience this abundant stage in my life. I had imagined this level to be many things but what I learned was that it was beyond my expectations. This phase has become about peace and understanding and how the universal energy really works and how to let it work for me. You are always in control of your own life and when you decide what it is that you want, whatever your Awesome Source is, you have to believe and trust in the process to take you there. No fear, no doubt, just pure belief you will bring it into your life, and you will.

When I went through the Struggle, fear had a grip on me and I hesitated in believing that manifesting would even work but I knew I had to give it my best shot, or I would never truly know. You see, you always have Awesome Source times, but without really seeing each stage with clarity, you can't fully appreciate this flow of abundance. As you hold it, the fear of losing it creeps in and it's gone again.

As I sit here writing this, my life situation is completely different to when I was writing Little Luxuries. I didn't want to write this chapter until I really wholeheartedly understood it. It's been almost a year until I finally felt ready to write. So much has changed for me. My marriage ended, I watched one of my best friends lose her battle with cancer and pass away way too young. She was younger than me and her passing had a profound effect that made me realise how precious time is. We don't know how long we have. I struggled mentally, emotionally, physically and spiritually during this time that took me through all the stages. Through that struggle I was able to really feel each one and work through it in a way that I never knew how.

Finding myself in Awesome Source shows me just how the universal source really works and how abundant it truly is. I often read about how we attract what we think, and I cannot confirm and stress that more to you, because yes, we do. Awesome Source is the place where you realise just how you allow this flow to happen. It's when it all feels like it aligns and you can actually see it happen before you. It's where you get a glimpse of how blessed and lucky you really are.

Whether its work/career, your love life, your health, your finances or even yourself as a person, peace and joy is found in Awesome Source and only you can take yourself there.

This love is not just around you but within you. The saying, 'You are the love you have been waiting for', is true – *you* are the love you have been waiting for.

How Do You Attract Awesome Source?

I always hear people say how difficult manifesting is and how they ask for what they want but it never comes. Manifesting to me is about aligning yourself to what it actually is that you want.

Thinking that alignment is just about 'you' can be where failure sets in. Sometimes creating what you want needs to align with another person, situation and energy.

Think about these possibilities.

If you are searching for love and you have put out to the universe what you want, the person you are looking for may not be ready for you. When clients ask me, how do I bring in the love I want, my answer is always to first love yourself, as that is the first barrier to break through. When you can love yourself, fully, completely, all your bumps and glitches, you are then ready to attract someone who will love you the same. If you don't have that to begin with, you will attract the love you have for yourself – finding someone who will see the faults you see in yourself and who will point out your insecurities or the things you don't like; someone who will treat you as you treat yourself, who will give you what you give yourself. When your self-worth is fractured, you may align with someone who can see what you see...get my point?

So loving, accepting and honouring yourself is the first BIG step!

It requires time and effort. Find an affirmation that works for you and say it, feel it and know it to be true. I started by looking in the mirror and saying to myself *every day*, 'I love and accept you just the way you are. You're beautiful, smart and infectiously funny and I am proud to be you.' Yes, every day!!! Even on the days I didn't love myself at all, I said it. I noticed that as I said it over and over again, it not only sunk in, but I started to believe it. Don't confuse it with an egotistic, full-of-yourself kind of love but a true deep love. The breaking point came a few days in when I truly looked into my eyes as I said the words and I broke down and cried. I realised how cruel I had been to myself, to my inner child. How I had ridiculed myself, told myself I deserved nothing good in my life and disliked everything about myself. That was such a pivotal moment for me. I realised that the little girl inside me was broken from not just what happened outside of her but what I was doing to her on the inside. I would never have said those things to anyone else, but I said it to myself. I knew that I had to change for her, for me.

I had to start way back. I found it hard to love myself as I was but seeing the little girl inside me who didn't love herself, drove me to make sure I did this right. I started with her. I saw that little five-year-old girl who had fear, lack of trust and sadness in her soul. I told her all the things she had wished she had heard. I had to gain her trust to pull her out of the dark hole she was stuck in. Over time, little by little, she felt my words of love and felt them to be true. She emerged a little at a time, we both had to believe and trust in each other. In time, during my affirmation, I felt her in my heart and I knew that she was out of the dark and was happy. Working on self-love for me had to start from the beginning, where I was the most vulnerable, when fear was a major part of my life. It was the place where I really needed that love, trust, and reassurance. I needed to find that moment in time when I went from being a happy little three-year-old girl to being totally consumed with confusion as to who I was and the life that surrounded me. Finding that moment was important as it was where the work had to begin. I had to trust in myself, believe that I had my own back and know that I loved myself enough to only want the best for myself. See the point now?

So if you are having trouble with self-love, find that little you, the one who didn't have self-confidence, that felt confused, hurt, not good enough, or even lonely. The one who didn't know who to trust or felt different to everyone else. Love that little you first. In time, you will see the 'now' you who stands before you in the mirror and love will be easy to find. Once you find that love, you can attract a love that will see what you see. Remember that just like you, someone is looking for that person too and that person always shows when you least expect it. The universe is 'surprising' like that.

When we want to manifest the work/career or finances in our lives, it comes when we let go of our fears with regard to them. I like to look at the fear, where it comes from and how it got there. You may find that someone that has financial problems has a fear of money or doesn't think they deserve it. It could be a past/inherited belief, something that was told to you by your parents, teacher, friend, or even a previous loss that has you on edge, fearing it might happen again.

I came to the edge. My fear of not having enough money was so strong that I nearly lost everything – my home and my life! I was so overwhelmed wondering how I could keep my head above water. I had been manifesting but I was manifesting with fear. So the universe continued to give me what I was afraid of. I was teaching others about manifesting but not practicing it appropriately myself.

The aha moment came when I actually questioned if my own manifesting in regard to money even worked! I manifested everything else but money. I would manifest and say, 'I don't need a lot and I don't want to be greedy so just give me what I need.' And you know what? They gave me what I needed – barely enough to keep my head above water – because I was continually giving myself limits since I didn't think I deserved it, because I didn't want to be selfish. But in the long run I was denying myself. The universe is abundant energy and here I was setting limits.

I had to find where this belief came from. My parents came to Australia in the 1960s from Italy. They barely had any money as they were also sending money home to their parents as well as trying to make a life in Australia. Sometimes dinner was bread and cheese. I didn't mind, I loved bread and cheese as a kid and still do, but I didn't realise at the time it was because they didn't have much money. I didn't have any toys because they couldn't afford them. I had a rusted tricycle that I barely rode but I had music. Music was my favourite. I had a record player and two singles that I played over and over. 'Things' have never mattered to me. I learned to live life with little money, few possessions/toys and little in my life. So I linked all that together. Deep down I learned to forgo things and I learned you had to work hard for everything. Money was only for the rich and not for me. My dad said to me that we come from poverty so our life will always be one of not having money. It stuck in my mind. I knew I had to change this point.

I started with my affirmation, 'I am free to live this life with no financial limits. Thank you for all the abundance that flows to me. My arms are wide open.'

When you ask, believe. Put your faith in you. Know that you are this magnet that will attract what you ask for as it flows past because you have no fear clouding that magnet. When we ask, it comes because we are ready, not because we want it. So if it's not coming, you are not aligned yet, you're not ready. Sometimes it comes at the last moment, but it comes.

The universe is abundantly magnificent. When you are in Awesome Source, you believe this to be true. Ask, Believe, Faith, Receive.

Chapter 12

HELP YOURSELF IN AWESOME SOURCE

These are the simple tools I use when I need guidance from the universe, God and my angels.

ASK, BELIEVE, FAITH, RECEIVE

ASK – For what you are wanting.
BELIEVE – Believe that you have been heard.
FAITH – Have faith that the answer will come.
RECEIVE – The answer you have asked for.

Yes, it is that simple, it just gets complicated with expectation. In this instant world we live in, we want everything yesterday. We have become impatient and we are becoming accustomed to receiving what we want, instantly!

The universe can work like that too. Sometimes you may be ready but other influences may not be aligned. Sometimes you may be ready to be in a loving relationship but the person you will align with is not. So whilst you wait, love yourself, they will come when the timing is good for both of you. No amount of pushing or stressing will make it happen sooner.

You may want a job in a workplace you have been dreaming about but there are no vacancies now, so enjoy the job you are in. When timing aligns, that job you have been wanting will come.

Not everything comes when only you are ready. If it includes someone or something else when you ask, you need to believe that your wish is out there and has been heard. You need to have faith that it is coming, and be ready when it does.

You have to surrender yourself to just knowing it will happen.

MEDITATION

Meditation is the bridge that connects you to the universe, so when you meditate, you raise your vibration to meet this energy where the universe (energy, God, angels, spirit guides, gods, etc.) communicates with you.

Find a quiet place where you can be silent and clear your mind. Let go of all the noise in your thoughts and just be. Meditation heightens your awareness. Switching your mind off to everything that is going on around you helps you to meditate effectively and recharge your soul.

FOUR SIMPLE WAYS THE UNIVERSE COMMUNICATES WITH YOU

The universe has four main ways of communicating with you. It can happen at any time and is heightened through meditation. It's about just pausing, being still and present in the moment. This gives you space where you can hear the whispers, see visions, feel and know the signs and messages you are being given by your god, angels, spirit guides, universal energy, gods, or whomever you connect to.

Clairvoyance – Clear Seeing

This is when you can see your sign or message. This can be in your mind's eye, in a dream, or seeing something out of the corner of your eye. Artists can paint from a vision in their mind, they can see it in a thought, as you would see it in your mind if you thought of an event that you can perceive in your mind.

Clairaudience – Clear Hearing

This is when your sign or message is heard. This can be from your higher self, that 'little voice inside'. You may hear a message in the lyrics of a song, or voices you can hear, or even your name being called.

Clairsentience – Clear Feeling

This is when your sign or message is felt. This is when our gut tells us if something feels good or not. Trust it! It may come as empathy, where you feel the emotions of others. You can feel good or bad vibrations about situations around you and you can feel universal energy.

Claircognisance – Clear Knowing

You just know a sign or message when you get it. You know it logically, and there is no explanation of how you can know it. It may come as an idea out of the blue. You know when someone is lying to you and you know something is right without knowing the facts. Trust it!

GETTING OUT IN NATURE

There is something about being outside in nature! Breathing in the fresh air, listening to the sounds of the wind, the trees, the birds and nature. This can be a form of meditation. If you are near the beach, feel the sand between your toes or stand on the grass and feel it under your feet. Being outside in nature strengthens your intuition. It grounds you.

WRITING/JOURNALLING

Write in a journal each day. Release your worries, take your thoughts out of your mind and onto paper so you don't have them swimming around in your head. Write your aspirations, your dreams, and let your creative juices flow, either through poetry, starting a novel or channelling your life experiences on paper. Also, write questions and see if you are ever guided to write answers. This is called 'automatic writing'.

PAY ATTENTION

When you ask for an answer, sign or message, pay attention. When you seek answers, be open to receiving the message. No point asking and then ignoring the world around you.

MAKE NOTE OF REPETITIVE MESSAGES & NUMBERS

When you pay attention to life around you, and you ask for messages and they are given, notice if they are repetitive.

Write them down as they will mean something to you, and in time they are always revealed. You could be receiving an answer but you are ignoring or doubting it, so you keep getting confirmation. Pay attention, take notice of these reoccurrences and know that there may be a hidden meaning that will be the answer you are waiting for.

Sometimes people notice synchronicities of numbers. For example, 11, 111, 222. Meanings of more common repetitive numbers are:

> **111** The universal wake-up call! Notice your thoughts, you are in heightened manifesting time, you are creating your thoughts so keep those thoughts on what you *do* want. This is a positive number to see and it tells you that you are on the right path so don't stop!
>
> **222** This has to do with relationships. Pay attention to those around you, people who are coming into or going out of your life. Stop worrying because everything is just as it should be. If this has come up with a new relationship, the universe is trying to tell you that this relationship is important so be careful and make sure there is balance.
>
> **333** This is the number for mind, body and spirit. Keep this in balance. If you are seeing this number, the universe is wanting you to have balance and one part of your life is taking over the others. Bring balance back into your life. This is also the number for Ascended Masters, so the big teachers are working with you! You have big things to learn!

444 This is about your tribe. One of your loved ones many need you so check in on them. This number also tells you that your angels want you to know they are surrounding your right now. They are here to support and guide you. You are not alone.

555 Opportunities are coming!! Change is in the air so don't be afraid of it, be prepared. Change means you're ready to step up. You can do it!

666 Reconnect with your god, angels, the universal energy as you need to refocus. You may have lost sight of your spiritual path.

777 You are most definitely on the right path, keep going and keep doing what you are doing!

888 The number of 'abundance'! Financial abundance is on its way! You are aligned to receiving.

999 Feeling Stuck? Universe is nudging you to finish something you started. You can do it, just get back on track and finish it because it will unlock the next adventure for you.

000 New beginnings BABY! A fresh start and this is the beginning you have been waiting for, and the universe has brought this to you.

DON'T OVER COMPLICATE THE SIGNS

Don't become obsessed with signs. People get lost in the search, so just be. When we search too hard, we see less and we doubt more. The universe has a way of showing you signs and repeats them if you don't get them. Don't question when the guidance comes in. Listen to your moral compass – if it feels right, just do it!

ENERGY WORK

When we are opening up to universal energy, we may be clogged up so that we can't see a sign even if it hits us in the face! I see it like we have gunk over our energy that we haven't cleared away. It's like a dirty aura. How can anything get in when we are blocked? Reiki makes me feel connected to the universal energy. I have used it as an energy cleaner and not just for healing.

Other great energy clearers are: tai chi, yoga, shamanic healing and many others.

SOUND WORK

Sound therapy is amazing for your energy, and certain sounds can transport you into a meditative state where you feel more connected with the universal energy. One of my favourite sound healings was at the Pyramids of Chi in Ubud Bali where the gongs, drums and sounds were very therapeutic. Find a sound therapy venue near you and give it a try.

USE ORACLE CARDS

Oracle cards are a great way to connect with your angels, gods, spirit guides and the universe. When you ask for guidance, you are drawn to the right cards and message that is important for you. Sometimes you can receive the same card, take notice of it, as this is the way you are receiving messages. Remember the universe is always trying to talk to you, so this is a tool that can help you get the guidance you need

AWESOME SOURCE AFFIRMATION EXERCISE

Say these affirmations out loud.
Emphasise the words most important to you.

My energy is entwined with the universal energy.
The universe listens to my energy and responds.
I have become *the me* I have always wanted to be.
I am transforming old energy into new energy.
I know who I am and what I am capable of.
I am co-creating every experience

When you finish saying these affirmations, I want you to close your eyes and with each big breath in say or visualise what you want to bring into your life. With each breath out say or visualise what you are letting go of.

Some examples:

Awesome Source Affirmations

Breathe in	***Breathe out***
I love my life	I let go of negativity
I am in tune with the universe	I let go of confusion
I create miracles	I let go of my mistakes
I am at present in my life	I let go of doubt

Awesome Source is being a part of the universal energy and moving together in synch. As you use the affirmations, let them help you become more connected to yourself, those around you, the environment and the life you are living. As you flow with life and enjoy the moments of being joyful, know that all of this works together. Work in harmony with life.

Become the you that you have always wanted to be.

YOUR AWESOME SOURCE JOURNAL

Write a time when you have been in the beautiful space of Awesome Source and how you felt in this space. How does it feel to be connected to yourself, your feelings and the universal energy?

This is your space to share your own journey.

Chapter 13

FREELY MOVING BETWEEN ALL LEVELS

As you see, these levels have their destructive and constructive aspects. When you are aware of the constructive ways, you will begin to see every level as a place where you can grow, learn and become more of the person you have always wanted to be.

Your foundation is your own belief system upon which your life is built. As you change your own beliefs, your life continues to change and attract what you believe you are worthy of, capable of, and surrounds you with a life that fits your perspective.

The Basement gives you self-care time. It helps you sink into your own space and be comfortable with that stillness. In this space, you can energise your body, mind and spirit so you can be stronger to face whatever comes your way. When life gets hard, let this place be your safety, your home, a place where you can hibernate and find peace. Remember, beauty is created down here – hit songs, poetry, paintings. Make this place work for you.

Sometimes you need to just get through the day choosing to be a robot and mechanically exist until you realise what you are striving for. Being in the Robot level can really help you get things done. Instead of pressuring yourself to make decisions, give yourself a little time to do what you need to do, but make sure you give yourself boundaries. Set a time limit for a goal so you don't get lost in here. When you believe that you are ready to do the work, take that leap where the Struggle begins.

The Struggle brings you from your knees to your feet. It's when you decide that you want more than the Robot could offer you. You are ready to take that leap, but you know that past pain needs healing. Any loose ends from past relationships, friendships, words that may have hurt you or things you may have said or done, these all need to be seen with clarity so you can help yourself let go. Instead of going back to the excuse you keep telling yourself – the bookmark in your story that you keep re-reading, or the pain you keep putting yourself through with a memory – go back and understand everyone's intentions. When we see it from all points of view, we can let it go. Trust in who you are and what you stand for.

Gratitude changes the world we live in! It really does. When we can see all of Life's Little Luxuries that surround our every moment, how we see the world and how the world sees us changes. Whether it hurt you or made you happy, being grateful for what it taught you can change your circumstances, from living a victim life, to being free. Know that all your trials, past pain and losses have led you to here. Be grateful that these experiences came along and forced you to change, and if you see change as an opportunity to better your life, be grateful for it. When you can see Life's Little Luxuries, you evolve and grow a little taller, wiser, humbler and happier.

The Awesome Source surrounds us every day, from the air we breathe to the blood that flows through our veins, we are here and connected. When we believe in the process of life, and we trust and know that we are connected and that our words are not only heard but felt, we change and become who we have always wanted to be. Our questions are answered, we see the visions materialise and we cherish the flow of goodness that enriches our lives. From the miracle of a baby, to the rising and setting sun, you are a part of this universe and we are one.

As you continue to flow through all these levels in life, you will change continuously. Sometimes changes are quick, sometimes they take longer but know that you will stop evolving when you are no longer living. You can fight against change, but if it's meant to be, it will be! Understanding these levels will help you flow. Work on your belief system, and use the levels to teach you, not scare you.

As I evolved, I began to notice the changes that were happening inside of me. I could hear my inner voice saying 'No' to something I didn't want to do, and I would flow with it and verbally say, 'No, no thank you'. I began to form boundaries and listen to my own needs that kept getting ignored when I was existing in the Robot level. I took better care of myself mentally, emotionally, physically and spiritually.

Changes don't just affect you, they affect everyone around you. As your energy evolves into something new, it begins to tune in to the next step in your journey. Others are connected to your journey when they don't feel threatened by it – they don't feel left out, they feel happy for you – so they take the journey with you.

As you evolve, there are others who don't like the new energy you are emitting, they won't like who you are or have become. I know this is hard because we all want to be liked and accepted but it's okay, not everyone is supposed to like you. Do you like everyone? These people can be friends, family or work colleagues. They are threatened by this 'new you'. The more self-confident, happy and content you are, the more others may feel uncomfortable because you may not be the obedient robot anymore. They become fearful, they become afraid because what you are mirroring back to them they don't know or understand. They won't understand how you are feeling; they won't know the hard work it took you to get here, the tears and pain, they just won't get it. All they will see is the change. People who want the best for you, want you to be at your best. Surround yourself with your tribe that fills your cup.

Your tribe will be by your side because they love you and are happy to see you not struggling with your life, seeing you actually having a dream and aspiring to follow it. But be aware that there are others who are not. Know that this journey is yours, and they are on their own journey. If they choose to step back, in your heart, send them love, and understand we are all on our own journey. Some people cross our paths for a reason. They have come to help you or you to help them. They may come to teach you a difficult lesson to help you grow. Once that help is complete, they leave. Some come to us for a short time. They may bring you joy, happiness and show you what love is. They may help you have faith in the world, and as quickly as they came, they left, but we will always cherish them.

Then there are those who come into our lives for a lifetime, they are the tribe. They are the ones who are there for you to lean on through thick and thin, the ups and downs. They support you and you support them. These are your people. Cherish them.

As you evolve, you are shedding your old skin, and starting to show your new fresh skin. You will be finding your feet in this new place of awareness so be gentle with yourself. Take each new step courageously, confidently and knowing you are fully supported. You have your back, and your tribe has your back.

If you are now in a place that finds you ready to take your leap of faith, hold your head up high; in your mind see your DREAM. In your heart, BELIEVE in this dream. In every cell of your being, TRUST in who you are. EVOLVE and BECOME the you that you have always wanted to be.

This is your life, your dream, your creation. Shine your Magnificence!

Always believe the best is yet to come!

ACKNOWLEDGEMENTS

I am very blessed to have had a number of people who have supported my dream to spread my vision and story globally.

My beautiful children Christopher and Danielle who continue to be my driving force to be the best I can be for myself. I am grateful to their spouses Emma and Sean that support and love them. My gorgeous grandson Thomas, who is my light, my sunshine and hope. I can't wait for more grandchildren!

I am thankful for my parents who have taught me so much about life. They have guided me to be a better version of myself. I have always wanted to make them proud, and it makes me happy to see it on their faces, that they are.

I am blessed to have many beautiful friends in my life that are family, you all know who you are. So many to mention but I thank you all from the bottom of my heart for supporting and loving me just as I am. No matter what, you have all stood by me, through thick and thin, and came out the other end!

To the many teachers along the way, I couldn't have learnt as much as I have without you. Some guided me, some challenged me, but in the end without you I wouldn't be here. Thank you.

I am especially grateful to Rob, who made me endless teas and made sure I had all I needed whilst I created and re-created this book. His love and kindness gave me that extra nudge I needed on days that I felt overwhelmed. He has been my cheerleader from the sidelines, reinforcing his belief in me and going to all extents to making sure I felt supported and loved. We grow when we are loved, nourished and looked after. Thank you for taking care of me Rob, you are the gift the universe has given to me.

I love you all so very much.

CPSIA information can be obtained
at www.ICGtesting.com
Printed in the USA
BVHW051028291021
620251BV00012B/259

9 780648 598817